Holiday Hilarities

a

Collection of Holiday Humor

by

Warren Dixon, Jr.

FIVE HAWKS

Five Hawks Press   Liberty, N.C.

ISBN 0-9648321-1-9

Library of Congress Catalog Card Number 98-93402

Printed in the U.S.A.

Cover and book design by Joyce Parham Design

Five Hawks Press
P.O. Box 1203
Liberty, N.C. 27298

To My Parents

Bertene and the late Dewey Dixon
Who instilled in me a love of Christmas

"The holiest of all holidays are those
Kept by ourselves in silence and apart;
The secret anniversaries of the heart."

-Longfellow

"If everyday were a holiday," said Willard,
"we would never grow old."
"Then you and I," I told him, "should live forever."

In Retrospect

Never having written a book, I didn't know what to expect when I self-published my first one, *Tarheel Hilarities*, in 1995.

Henry King, famed author and former columnist for the Asheboro *Courier-Tribune*, said it was like birthing a baby.

Buck Paysour, fishing book author and former feature columnist for the Greensboro *News and Record*, said it was a wonderful road to bankruptcy. But, he added, it would also be like a second job.

It seemed like the thing to do to me, a sort of childhood dream. I guess if you're going to write, it's a logical progression: you write, you publish, you starve.

When I first mentioned to my friend and banker Charlie Bowen that I would probably be needing a substantial loan to publish a book and that I had some misgivings about the whole project, he asked me a question.

"What is the worst thing that can happen?" he wanted to know.

I said, "Bankruptcy, divorce, a pauper's burial, ridicule from what friends I haven't alienated through my column in the paper, scorn from my critics..."

He was curious that I had friends left that I hadn't alienated through my column.

"You've alienated Larry Penkava, columnist for *The Randolph Guide* and you've never even met him," he said.

"I've run out of people I know," I admitted.

Then he said something I'll always remember:

"But you'll have the satisfaction of fulfilling a life-long dream. You don't get many chances of fulfilling a dream."

So I published *Tarheel Hilarities* and I've never once regretted it. The book has since taken on a life of its own and, in turn, introduced me to some incredible people.

I owe a debt of gratitude to Bill Flynn and Leanne Petty of WMAG Radio who gave me my first interview; to Stan Swofford of the Greensboro *News and Record* and Steve Huffman of the *High Point Enterprise*; to Bob Branard, Martha Hundley and Margarette Sheppard who almost bought my entire stock of books among them; to Chip Womick of the Ramseur *Bulletin*; to Milburn Gibbs of the *Chatham News* (and now the editor of the *Liberty News*); and to the staff of Atticus Books, an independent bookstore that is now gone but not forgotten.

Beverly Wilson of "Picture This" in Liberty, N.C., hosted my first book signing, a very special time, and I will always be grateful to her. While at this first signing, Helen Loflin told me her sister had been cured of shingles while reading my columns. Is laughter the best medicine or what?

So, if a few columns will improve your health, what will a whole book do? Or, in this case, two books.

Preface

Anyone who has ever untangled Christmas lights only to have them blow out like popcorn when plugged in is bound to appreciate the humor of the holidays. I know a holiday brings much joy to my life, whether it's trying to straighten out a crooked Christmas tree or cook hamburgers for fifty Fourth of July guests on a ten dollar grill.

Many of our holidays had pagan beginnings and probably would be more suitably celebrated today if we could just make a few human sacrifices beforehand, preferably a boss or two or some in-laws. But we are saddled with cumbersome laws and have to abide by them.

So, about all we have left is to suffer through the holidays, then to laugh at them afterwards. I hope this book brings you some of those laughs. That's my main reason for writing, to make you laugh.

Many of the stories that make up this book originally appeared as columns in the Ramseur (N.C.) *Bulletin*, although they have been re-written. My thanks to editor Chip Womick and publisher Bob Derr for allowing me to reprint them here.

Others are new and have never been published before, including "The Joy in the Morning Club", "The Christmas Cabin", "Biltmore", "Christmas Encyclopedia", "The Party", "Christmas Letters", "Dreaming of a Slushy Christmas", and "Wisemen's Wives".

Some of these stories are based on the truth. Some are entirely fiction. The rest fall somewhere in between.

Let me apologize to all my regular readers for the length of "The Joy in the Morning Club". I know how short your attention span is and how you like to read one little three-page story at a time while sitting on the john. But try to stick it out and finish the whole thing. I've split it up into short segments to try to help you out so if you fall asleep (like most of you do) while reading it you can pick it back up the next night.

Many thanks to my wife Sandra for not only looking after the yard while I put together another book but also for support, encouragement and advice. My gratitude to Sandra, stepdaughters Julie and Jamie and friends Willard and Sue Lynn, Hoyle, Walt and Susan Foster and Ed and Peggy Christenbury for doing crazy things so I can write about them. A special thanks to Debbie Hinshaw of BB&T who financed this project, to Joyce Parham of Julian N.C. who designed the cover and to authors Henry King and Buck Paysour, who are my inspiration.

Contents

The Joy in the Morning Club

Christmas wasn't Christmas, Grandma said, without friends, family and a little wine. And not always in that order, she added.

Myrtis nodded, sipped some wine from her jelly glass, wiped her chin, then asked the same question for the thirteenth time: "Where am I and who are you people?"

It was Christmas Eve, 1959, a long time ago in days and years, but in my mind it is just as clear as the day before yesterday. Yet to understand the events of that day, we have to go back a few months before that Christmas, to the summer of 1959. You wouldn't think Christmas could start in the heat of the summer, but you must understand that Christmas is always in our hearts, ready, like Ned the dog, to spring at any moment.

Ned the dog (Ned the butt-biting dog as Willard called him) patiently waited that July day in 1959, crouched between the holly bushes near the back door of Willard's grandma's house. Years of experience had taught Ned that the back door was the way we would leave the house and the holly bushes, although scratchy, offered him the best vantage point to jump us when we came out.

It was one of those days in Piedmont North Carolina when the air stuck to you like fly paper. Inside the house it was no cooler, just more hot air moving courtesy of a window fan in the living room.

"It must be a hundred degrees in here," I heard Willard's mom mutter. "My makeup is running down my face like lava." Willard's mom, Nadine, was not a happy woman. Her slip was clinging to her like Saran Wrap, her face was beginning to look like a Zebra and her father was lying dead at Moffitt's Mortuary. And right after supper she'd found what seemed like a nation of ants living in her mother's kitchen cabinet, a discovery that made her back itch badly. There was a time when her mother would not have tolerated one ant, much less a whole herd of them. But the ants would have to wait until we returned from the funeral home.

Willard's grandpa had died the day before, an event that had been expected for some time. The old man had suffered a massive stroke that morning while eating a breakfast of country ham, red eye gravy, biscuits, brains and eggs and butter milk. His last words had been "Lord, how I do love these cracklings."

Willard's grandma (we all just called her "Grandma") had been predicting his death for twenty years, citing his poor eating habits which she was sure had led to high blood pressure, clogged arteries, and a myriad of other health problems.

"I told him he was killing himself," Grandma said the day he died. "No one could live on a diet like that, all that fatback and buttermilk. His veins must have been clogged up worse than my kitchen sink."

The fact that Grandpa had just turned 90 did not hold much weight with Grandma. She was certain that if he'd watched his diet, exercised regularly instead of fox hunting all night long, he could have lived at least as long as Methuselah.

Nadine came out of a back bedroom in a black print dress. Her hair was already frizzing. Willard and I were sitting in the living room, neckties like nooses around our necks, about as comfortable as alley cats in tuxedos.

"Come on ya'll," she said, "we're late already. Sam's waiting on us."

Sam was Willard's dad who was already in the car, no doubt listening to the radio and smoking a Pall Mall.

"Be sure to flip the porch light on," Nadine told Willard. "It'll be dark by time we get home."

Ned the dog had undoubtedly seen this four-in-a-row alignment many times during his career, first as a spaniel and first class bird hunter and then in his later years as a champion butt-biter. The old woman in the front he recognized immediately as the one who fed him daily and rubbed him fondly between the eyes occasionally. He would not bite her out of respect. We two skinny boys in the middle provided a poor target with little meat on our bones and besides, Ned had once bitten the man in the middle and been rewarded by a kick from the person behind. No, he knew well the one to latch onto was the last one in the procession.

He waited until Nadine passed by the holly bush and then bounced out, nipping her on the rear before she knew what was happening. As she whirled around, slinging her rather imposing pocket book at him, his front foot caught her hose and left a long red scratch down her leg along with a rip in her nylons from her thigh to her ankle.

Nadine was at first speechless and could only muster an abbreviated kick at Ned as he headed for the safety of the barn. She let out a yell about the time he disappeared behind the shed. He had done his duty for the day.

"That Ned's lucky he ducked that satchel," Willard's Dad said as we crawled into the car. "As much as that thing weighs, he'd be one dead dog if it'd hit him."

Nadine slung the pocket book again, except this time it found its target at the center of the back of Sam's head. He was quiet the rest of the way to the funeral home.

I don't mean to make light of Willard's grandpa's death. We were all sad to see the old man go, even Grandma who had rode him like a wet dog most of his life. Although she harped at him constantly about his eating habits and his ragged hunting coat that smelled like fox hounds we knew deep down she loved him because we had seen them holding hands before.

The funeral home was much more like a party than a funeral. Jack Ledwell would have wanted it that way, though, and had even said that if he ever did die he wished everyone would sit around, laugh, drink a little wine and tell some tales of days gone by.

That was exactly what they did, most of them acting like Jack Ledwell's corpse didn't exist, others casting a wary eye toward the casket as they passed by it. There wasn't any wine drinking, though, except in the parking lot, although there were a lot of tales told, some of them true.

Jack Ledwell may have been dead, but his memory lived on in the minds of his friends.

Humped over Ben Cooper told of staying out with Jack and Rufus Cole on an all night fox hunt, then plowing fields the entire next day behind mules. Jack Ledwell had told him a few days before he died that he didn't think they could do that again.

"We could fox hunt all night," he had laughed, "but I don't think we could manage the plowing."

The preacher recalled asking Jack to come to church more often.

"The weather's pretty," Jack had said, "and the fish are biting. God and I can talk plenty down by the pond. And anyway, after the fox hunting and the fishing's over, God and I'll have plenty of time together."

"I got a feeling," the preacher said, "that if Heaven has a pond, God'll find Jack beside it wetting his hook."

Rufus Cole remembered the Christmases and how much Jack Ledwell enjoyed them.

"He always wanted to have one big Christmas party with all his friends," Rufus said, "but we were always all too busy with our families."

It was sometime during all this story telling that Grandma broke down and cried. None of us had ever seen Grandma cry, not even when she slammed her thumb in the car door. It was an occurrence so unexpected that Nadine sat down with her arm around Grandma for a long time. When she stood up she had decided that Willard and I, although only thirteen years old each, should stay with Grandma "until she got back on her feet."

As Willard's dad said later "it was a lot like leaving the rats to look after the cheese," although he didn't say it in earshot of Nadine, his head still smarting some from her pocket book.

When we got back to the old farm house, Nadine sent Willard and I in as guinea pigs, Willard having forgotten to leave the porch light on. Ned was nowhere to be seen, though, and we all made it into the house unscathed.

That night as we'd settled into our beds, Ned could be heard barking furiously down near the barn. We all knew we were safe, because Ned only barked at friends and family.

❦

That was how Willard and I came to stay with his grandma Mattie Ledwell for awhile and how we got to know the ladies in the Joy in the Morning Club.

The Joy in the Morning Club was made up only of widow women, that's how Grandma got into it. Her friend

Elsie Martin had called Grandma not too long after Jack Ledwell died to invite her to a meeting. As Willard's dad said, it gave the ladies something to do, there being a big void in their lives not having their husbands' affairs to run anymore.

The main purpose of the club, it seemed to Willard and me, was for the ladies to gather at each other's homes and discuss which stores had the best specials on dish washing detergent that week. But it ended up being much more than a gathering of gossipy old women, a fact that became very apparent to us that Christmas.

Elsie Martin had founded the club several years before after her husband had passed away suddenly one Wednesday night. According to Willard's dad, Mr. Martin had died a horrid death, having become asphyxiated on fumes while Elsie was giving herself a home permanent.

Elsie Martin, along with Myrtis Beane, Clovis Beachum and Pearl Nelson formed the heart of the Joy in the Morning Club. It was difficult for the ladies to get used to life after their husbands passed away and they all coped differently.

Pearl Nelson, for instance, had been so afraid to stay by herself that it was feared for awhile, especially by her daughter-in-law, that she would move in with her son in Sedalia. Pearl discovered her husband's old .38 Special revolver, however, stuck it in her nightstand and this seemed to give her the courage she needed to live alone. Later she realized that she had no ammunition for it and begged her son to buy her some. Afraid that his mother would shoot her foot off some night, he purchased her blanks instead.

Clovis Beachum's son Lynwood still lived at home with her and she spent much of her time looking after him. Lynwood worked at the local Western Auto.

Clovis worried about Lynwood constantly. In high school he had been voted most likely to die in a motel room alone. He must have been thirty or forty, still living at home. The living at home part was OK with Clovis, but she worried about him nevertheless and prayed for him every day. Lynwood, however, attributed any luck he was having to the mystical numbers he recited daily.

Myrtis Beane found solace in her church after her husband passed away and was on so many committees that she sometimes missed the Joy in the Morning meetings. She often proudly told the ladies of the club how religious her husband had become in his later years just before his death.

"I figure," grandma told her, "that old age took care of what religion got credit for."

Elsie Martin took up patriotism as a hobby after her husband's death. He had been a company clerk in Maryland during World War I and according to Elsie, had been instrumental in bringing the war to an early close. Grandma always said that Mr. Martin had died of a "cerebral hemorrhoid".

Grandma said Elsie was the most patriotic person she'd ever met.

"I'll bet if she was sitting on the commode and they played The Star Spangled Banner, she'd stand up," Grandma noted.

Willard and I decided that even if she did, it was not something we wanted to know about.

And then there was Grandma, at whose big rambling farm house the ladies most often met. Grandma, as Willard's dad said, was "so tight she wouldn't pay a dime to see an earthquake." But after she got into the Joy Club she loosened up a bit and often made cakes for the group.

The ladies met about once a week, sometimes more, at each other's homes and shared the latest gossip, ate desserts and sometimes, for health purposes only, drank a little wine. Every now and then, they'd take field trips downtown or to the grocery store or a nearby restaurant. You've got to remember, this was back at a time when it was not illegal to drink and drive. As a matter of fact, it was encouraged.

Nadine was glad that Grandma had learned to drive earlier in her life, an enthusiasm Willard and I didn't share. It gave Grandma freedom she wouldn't have otherwise, Nadine reasoned. Willard and I figured it just put one more highly dangerous hazard on the road.

Like the time she drove us, at a top speed of five miles an hour, to the Speedy Chicken and tried to order our food through the garbage can instead of the drive-through speaker. Or the day she bent the "no parking" sign back double in the grocery store parking lot.

"Don't worry," she told us. "It'll straighten back up when we leave. It always does."

And we never were really sure how much Grandma could see. She had lost an entire pack of hotdog weenies one night while cooking supper and never found them. We'd even looked in the washing machine for them. And she had driven into a ditch one day trying to pull out of the service station. The attendant had come over and tapped on her window and told her that she was in the ditch. Willard and I noticed the car was sitting at an odd angle, but we just figured she'd rammed something again and knocked the car whoppy-jawed.

One day after Nadine had seen Grandma leading a convoy of cars, pickups and transfer trucks into town at five miles an hour, she suggested to Grandma that she might want to speed up some. That's how we got to meet Sgt. Nelson.

Sgt. Nelson, he said later, thought surely when he turned the siren on, the white car with the black scars down the side would pull over. Willard and I, sitting in the back, had already seen the police car behind us with its red lights flashing, but Grandma and Elsie were in such an animated conversation that they must've missed it.

And Sgt. Nelson had later admitted that he thought the car might be rolling out of control, since he could see no sign of a driver. Grandma was so small that her head didn't stick up over the seat and she looked through the steering wheel to see to drive.

Finally we pulled into the driveway at Grandma's and stopped. Sgt. Nelson put his hat on and got out of his patrol car. This is when Grandma spotted him for the first time.

"Good morning, ladies," he said after Grandma had rolled down the window. He gave Willard and I a quick glance and evidently saw no harm in us, because he took his hand off his holster and leaned with his right hand against the car.

"May I see your driver's license and registration card, ma'am?"

"Oh, my," said grandma in her most polite voice. "Have I done something wrong?" She began searching the front seat for her pocket book. "Elsie, did I leave my pocket book at the grocery store?"

"Why didn't you stop when I turned on the red light and siren?" he asked, as she searched for the elusive purse.

"I thought you always rode around with them on," she replied.

"Are you Pearl Nelson's boy?" Elsie asked, leaning over grandma to get a better look at him.

"No, ma'am, she's my aunt. I'm Ross's boy."

"Pearl's in the Joy in the Morning Club," Elsie continued as if she hoped knowing Pearl would mitigate their sentence. "She's our best friend. We just love her to death."

The truth of the matter was they had just been talking about Pearl and how her dentures clicked like castanets, but neither I nor Willard was about to bring it up at the moment.

"Here's that pocket book," said Grandma, "in the back seat with the groceries. Now where is that license?"

"Here's mine," said Elsie helpfully.

"It has to be the driver's," said Sgt. Nelson.

"Ross Nelson," said Elsie, "he ran the Esso station over at Flint Hill, didn't he?"

"Here's my Sear's credit card," said Grandma, "will that do?"

"When did you get a Sear's credit card?" Elsie asked her. "I have tried and tried and they won't send me one. I don't think they want my business."

"Well, it wasn't hard to get, I just asked for it. They're glad for you to have it. Does Ross still run that Esso station?"

"Ma'am, do you know you were going 55 miles an hour down Cotton Mill Hill? That's a 35 mile an hour zone..."

"You can't give a policeman your Sear's credit card, Mattie," said Elsie. "It doesn't have your picture on it."

"Ma'am, you were speeding..."

"Well," Grandma said, "my daughter Nadine... she's the one who loaned me these boys in the back seat to look after me. That's my grandson and his friend. I don't hold it against her, though. Well, she told me if I was going to drive to speed it up some. She said I was holding up progress, I think that's how she put it. And Elsie here said you needed to air out your car now and then to blow the carbon out of it. I thought I could get a running start down the hill. I didn't realize I was doing anything wrong."

"Would you like to come inside and have some tea?" Elsie asked him. "It's mighty hot out here."

"It is hot," Grandma agreed, "I hope our ice milk hasn't melted."

"It was on special," said Elsie.

Sgt. Nelson wrote Grandma a warning ticket and gave her a short lecture on how speed kills and everything and how, if you wanted to blow the carbon out of your car, you needed to let a mechanic do it. Then he joined us for tea and cake, looking almost relieved to get the ordeal over with.

Grandma never did find her license in her pocket book, although she turned up some eye glasses she'd lost over a year before, part of a Moon Pie and a book she'd borrowed from the library that November.

🍂

Willard and I thought Grandma had hired a woman, a rather homely chunky woman, to mow her yard. We'd spotted her pushing the mower behind the barn near the fox hound lot one day. But Grandma denied it.

"I only hired Seymore and Little Tommy," she said. "Maybe Seymore brings his sister sometimes to help, but I've never seen her. He's always had Little Tommy with him when I've been here. If he's got a woman helping him, he hasn't told me. I'm not paying for three of 'em, I'll tell you that. I can barely afford two."

Seymore was a short, stocky fellow who did the mowing. As Grandma said, he was "the brains of the outfit." Little Tommy usually welded the sling blade and cut the weeds Seymore couldn't get to with the mower.

It was hard to tell how old Little Tommy was. He seemed to be slightly mentally retarded and always looked like he come directly from a coal mine. It was apparent that he'd not been around any soap for quite some time. His hair stood straight up like a shoe brush and he wore a bandana around his head when he helped Seymore. The bandana seemed to be more for fashion, although Willard said he thought it might serve to keep any sweat off Little Tommy's face, Tommy evidently being allergic to water in any form. He also wore his pants up around his armpits. Grandma said that was so if it flooded, Tommy wouldn't have to worry about getting his pants legs wet.

But Little Tommy had a gentleness about him that Grandma fondly fell in love with and when she brought them iced tea after they'd mowed, she'd always sneak him an extra cupcake.

We discovered who the mowing woman was one day when we overheard Grandma talking with Elsie as they sat at the kitchen table.

"I felt so sorry for Seymore," she was telling Elsie. "I know how hard it is to get into those hose in this hot weather."

"Hose?" Elsie asked incredulously. "Did you say hose?"

"Yes," said grandma. "He and Little Tommy were mowing the yard today and you know how hot it was. Well, I was watching them to make sure they mowed and didn't diddle."

"You don't pay them by the hour do you?" asked Elsie.

"No, but I don't like people to diddle. Well, I lost Seymore and didn't know where he went. I looked out the kitchen window here and saw him behind the pack house changing clothes."

"Changing clothes?" repeated Elsie.

"Yes," said Grandma, "and you know I don't see too well. So I pulled up a stool close to the window so I could get a better view."

"What was he doing?" asked Elsie incredulously.

"He was putting on his hose and you know how hot it is," replied Grandma. Elsie just sat there looking stunned.

"And he had these cute little panties," Grandma continued. "And the nicest skirt, although I wouldn't have mowed the yard in it. I'd sort of like to know where he got that skirt. I wonder where he shops."

"Do you think he's gay?" asked Elsie.

"Oh, he looked happy enough," Grandma answered. "Except for those high heel shoes. He finally had to take them off and put on some flats. You can't mow in high heels."

"I mean do you think he's, well, right?"

"Oh, I think he's all right, except for being pregnant."

"Pregnant," Elsie gulped, taking a sip of tea. "He's pregnant?"

"Yes," said Grandma, "and by the looks of him he's about due ."

"Do you think we ought to give him a baby shower?" Elsie asked.

"That would be nice," Grandma said, "but I don't think he's going to have a baby. I think it's a basketball.

" What would you buy for a basketball?"

It wasn't that Grandma didn't like Baptists. She just didn't trust them.

"They think they're the only ones going to Heaven," she always said. "There's a lot of us Methodists gonna be there, too. Well, a few anyway."

Grandma never missed a chance to aggravate the Baptists, which wasn't hard. We figured that was the main reason she moved the Mexicans into her rental house.

The Lilly family had lived in the old sharecropper's shack before the Mexicans. They moved in paying no rent for the first few months on the condition that they help Grandma out on the farm.

Grandpa was very little help anymore, as Grandma had pointed out to the clerk down at the Farmer's Alliance store one day when he asked how her husband was doing.

"Oh, he's dead," Grandma told him matter of factly.

The clerk stuttered his condolences and said he was sorry, he hadn't heard.

"Oh, you know," Grandma explained, "he still hangs around, he's just dead. Just as soon as he does die, I'm gonna look around the funeral home for me another man."

This, of course, was several years before Grandpa's actual death, but that was how Grandma always talked about him.

The Lilly family hadn't lived up to their end of the bargain on working out their rent and we all knew that Grandma was losing her patience with them. One afternoon as several of her Baptist neighbors were walking by, Grandma decided she'd had enough.

"Consider the Lillys in the field," she told them. "They toil not, neither do they spin."

That was the last we saw of the Lillys.

The next week the Mexican family moved in. Mind you, this was at a time when there were no different nationalities such as Mexicans or Yankees abounding in Piedmont North Carolina. Grandma came under immediate criticism for allowing the family to move into the neighborhood, especially among the Baptists.

Mrs. Dillard, wife of one of the deacons, contended that the Mexicans might have broken into her beauty shop.

"Whoever did it ought to be shot," she ranted. "They left an empty wine bottle right in the middle of the floor and got into my refrigerator and ate all my collard greens. Do you know how much trouble it is to fix collard greens? And my chickens keep getting gone. I think they're ending up as Mexican stew."

Grandma admitted that the collard stealing was probably a capital offense, but finally convinced Mrs. Dillard that the Mexicans wouldn't care for her collard greens.

"And I've never heard of Mexican stew," she assured Mrs. Dillard, although she later privately admitted to Elsie that she had once shared some chicken and rice with the old Mexican, Manuel Fernando Hermandez.

There was also a nasty rumor going around long before Grandpa's death about Grandma and Manuel, and how they had been seen together sitting on the stump near the corn crib. There wasn't any corn in the crib anymore, but everyone knew that was where Grandma kept her homemade strawberry wine. That was Grandma's main vice, the homemade medicinal wine she sipped whenever her stomach acted up. Her stomach had gotten progressively worse over the years, forcing Grandma to make the stuff by the gallon.

It was the day that Manuel brought his daughter, son-in-law and grandson to North Carolina that changed the whole community. Grandma went to meet them when the taxi dropped them off in front of the rental house and was introduced by the old man.

"How do you spell that name?" she asked, when told that the small grandson's name was "Hey-sus".

"J-e-s-u-s," Manuel wrote on a cardboard box.

"Jesus," repeated Grandma. "Jesus. Wait till Mrs. Dillard finds out Jesus is living next door to me."

Grandma was not a heathen, although she was an admitted Methodist. She did like her wine, though, especially after the doctor mentioned to her, off hand, that it was good for her stomach. Ever since then she had kept several bottles nearby just for that purpose and to our knowledge, had not had a stomach problem since. If she had, Willard said, a couple of glasses of wine later and she didn't seem to care.

One of the favorite activities of the ladies was eating. Several members of the Joy Club had expressed a desire to try out a new all you could eat restaurant in Ether. Except none of them wanted to drive that far and certainly none of them wanted to drive at night.

As Myrtis was heard to say "I can't even see the road in broad daylight, much less at night." This was consoling to us in that we had often ended up riding with her on these outings.

This is when Lynwood Beachum, Clovis's son, volunteered to drive us to Ether. Lynwood had just purchased a used van and was itching to drive it. He'd bought it from the Scrub Oak Baptist Church down at Biscoe and it still had "Scrub Oak Baptist Church" printed on the driver's door. Most people would have painted over the lettering, but not Lynwood. He seemed to enjoy the notoriety it brought him and the looks he got when he squealed the tires taking off at the stop light.

Willard and I were excited over the trip having gotten tired of eating rabbit three times a day lately. Grandma had discovered Jack Ledwell's rabbit gums and had set them around the fields near the house, hoping to catch some of the bunnies and save money on groceries. The rabbits were prolific and we had eaten fried rabbit, rabbit stew, rabbit pot pie and rabbit salad until our ears were starting to grow long and floppy. We figured rabbit-kabobs were next.

The ladies decided to take the trip on a Thursday afternoon after Lynwood got off work at the Western Auto. The trip down was uneventful, with Grandma wanting to sing "Ninety-nine bottles of beer on the wall", except that no one knew the words. We ended up singing "Row, Row, Row Your Boat," which suited Myrtis better, it not being, as she said "a heathern song."

We got to the restaurant and didn't have to wait long to get in. Willard and I ate banana pudding for our entree and topped it off with chocolate chip cookies and ice cream. The ladies, protesting that they couldn't eat this and that, nearly cleaned out the restaurant anyway and would have been asked not to come back if I had owned the place.

On the way home, we passed a Colonial Store and Grandma asked Lynwood to stop. She was nearly out of strawberry wine and wanted to buy a bottle or two. Pearl said she needed to buy a card for a friend.

"I know I can't find one," she said, "I need one of those 'I know you're not going to get well' cards and I bet they don't have one. All they have is those cheery Get Well Soon cards."

She and Pearl and Lynwood went in while the rest of us sat in the van and digested our food.

Grandma came back first with her wine. Grandma didn't buy just any wine. She always went with the new wine with the screw caps, not that old stuff with the corks. Nothing but the best for Grandma.

"The manager saw us pull up," she said as she crawled in the van. "And he saw me buying the wine. He wanted to know where our church was. Lynwood told him I was the minister of recreation."

Myrtis winced.

About that time we saw Pearl come out with her purse in one hand and her grocery bag in another. Except she headed west as she exited the store in the opposite direction from where we'd parked. Lynwood blew the horn at her, but she kept her eyes straight ahead and didn't stop until she saw a half dozen Mexicans sitting in a van.

Peering in the window of the van, she stared at the Hispanics. They, in turn, looked at her puzzeledly, then waved at her.

"What have you done with my friends?" she screamed, dropping her grocery bag. "Where's Mattie and Clovis and those two stupid boys?" Willard and I later thanked Pearl for her loyalty, but requested that next time she describe us a little more kindly.

"She's gone to the wrong van," Lynwood said.

Then, as we watched in amazement and Lynwood blew the horn, Pearl pulled her .38 Special revolver out of her purse.

"You are going to pay dearly for this," she stuttered, waving the gun nervously at the van. "Now what have you done with my friends?"

Suddenly all four doors flew open and six Hispanic men scrambled out of the van and ran in six different directions.

"You're lucky I didn't shoot you all," Pearl yelled after them.

"Pearl, over here," shouted Lynwood. Finally she saw us, put her gun away, picked up her groceries and returned to the correct van looking slightly confused.

"Remember, Annie Oakley," Grandma told her, "the next time you try to find our van, it's the one with 'Scrub Oak Baptist Church' on the door."

As we rode home we noticed an occasional Mexican jogging along the highway, looking frequently over his shoulder.

Willard and I were in the barn one morning having a corn cob fight when we spotted the prowler at the back of the house. He was a mean-looking character with a straw hat covering his long stringy hair, baggy overalls over what looked like a pink house coat, boots and a commode plunger in his hand. We watched in horror as he picked his way along the back of the house, peering in all the windows and trying to pry them open.

There was no telling, Willard said, how desperate a man might be who wore overalls over a pink housecoat and carried a commode plunger.

Of course, we had no way of knowing at the time that it was Grandma.

Grandma said later she had realized her mistake the moment the door from the kitchen to the back porch slammed shut. There she was locked out of her house in her house coat. She had no bra on, no shoes and hadn't even brushed her hair. Worse yet, she had left her teeth in a bowl beside the sink in the house.

Now, I wonder what I came out here for, she muttered to herself.

Grandma was not one to stand around feeling sorry for herself. Jack Ledwell had installed a small half bath on the back porch to wash up when he came in from the fields and that's where she headed. Sure enough, there was a spare set of dusty teeth on the sink in a dry bowl.

Oh, Lord, I hope they're mine, she thought as she washed them off and stuck them in her mouth. Then she looked around for some clothes. Over in the corner of the porch, she found a pair of Jack's overalls, an old hat and a pair of boots. She tucked her hair up on the top of her head and stuck the hat on over it and stepped into the overalls. When she put up her hair, she discovered her eye glasses and realized that was what she had come out on the porch looking for in the first place.

She searched the back porch for a key, but found none.

I'll have to go outside and try to crawl in a window, she thought. I can't let anyone know I'm this stupid. She grabbed a commode plunger thinking it might help loosen a window.

Grandma clumped outside in Grandpa's boots, and checked out each window in the house, but found none open. Hoping against hope, she rattled the front door. Locked tight. Then a horrible thought hit her, a circumstance worse than being locked out of her house. She hadn't made up her bed that morning. If her neighbors found that out, she would be the talk of the town. Especially that Elsie. Elsie, Mrs. Perfect Housekeeper, would never let her live it down.

Willard and I saw the small man in the baggy overalls and cap as he looked in the windows at the back of the house. We knew we had to do something fast, because the wiry fellow had a weapon, a commode plunger. There was no telling what he intended to do with that. Plus, by the way he weaved in his boots, he was obviously drunk. At first we thought about corn cobbing him to submission, but Willard said that he'd heard of people being plungered to death. So instead we decided to run as fast as we could to Elsie Martin's house to call the police.

Elsie, highly upset that Grandma was in trouble, called Sgt. Nelson the moment we told her what had happened. Then she attempted to dial Grandma to warn her of the approaching danger. There was no answer. We hopped in Elsie's car to go rescue Grandma.

Grandma heard the car coming down the road. Just my luck, she thought, someone will see me. She ducked into the bushes in front of the house.

Elsie Martin looked over toward grandma's house as she passed and thought she caught a glimpse of a man in overalls lurking under Grandma's window. She slowed her car and looked again. There he was, an evil looking man with a hat pulled over his eyes, hunched over in the yellowbell bush. Surely Sgt. Nelson would be there soon. She wished she had a gun like Pearl and made a promise to herself to get one.

We hadn't gone far when we met Sgt. Nelson in his patrol car barreling towards Grandma's. Behind him was a sheriff's car and following that was the entire local fire department.

Sgt. Nelson jumped from his car before it came to a stop and cornered the person behind the yellowbells.

"Stand up," barked Sgt. Nelson, "and come out of that bush."

"I am standing up," Grandma grunted.

After Grandma had explained her situation, Sgt. Nelson suggested calling Nadine, who had a spare key.

"You might as well," snorted Grandma. "And call News-8 , too. Everybody else is here, they might as well film it."

"Oh, my," purred Elsie, standing on the front porch looking in the window of Grandma's bedroom. "We haven't even made up our bed."

❦

The closer to Christmas, the more melancholy Grandma became. She couldn't seem to get Grandpa off her mind.

There were reminders of him everywhere. As you entered the house on the back porch, the first thing that caught your eye was the old fox hunting horn he'd made from a cow's horn and his hunting coat on a peg. All his tools were right where he'd last laid them. She'd open a drawer to look for a pair of scissors and find a pocket knife of his and she'd sit there for the longest time, gazing at it. She still kept his clothes in the closet, just like he'd left them. We'd find her in her favorite chair in a corner, looking at photograph albums for hours at a time.

All this created a strong presence of Jack Ledwell in the old farmhouse. You could feel it. It was as if he was trying to go but Grandma wouldn't let him. She was having a struggling time without him.

Willard and I were getting a little tired of staying at Grandma's and knew that our parents must've been desperate to get us back home again. It was a terrific sacrifice for them to loan us out to Grandma like they did. They seemed to hold up well without us, though, although we figured it was just an act. Willard said that deep down they must've been heartbroken.

We even feared that Willard's parents had had trouble with burglars since we'd been at Grandma's because we overheard Sam tell Nadine that "now was a good time to change all the locks" at the house.

No matter how much our parents needed us at home, we made a vow to stay with Grandma for the duration.

Thanksgiving came and went. Grandma had served roast rabbit, rabbit dressing, rabbit dumplings and for days afterwards, rabbit salad. I noticed that Willard had developed a pronounced hop in his walk. Then a few days after Thanksgiving Grandma announced her plans.

"I want all of us to have a giant Christmas party," she said. "For Jack. Jack would like that ."

The fact that Grandma talked about her late husband in the present tense bothered Willard and I. And late at night while we were lying in bed upstairs in the old farm house, we could hear talking downstairs. Willard said it was Grandma talking to Grandpa.

I hoped privately that he would talk her into varying her menu some, like maybe some fried chicken and gravy for a change.

Grandma had merely wanted to have a Christmas party, nothing more. And she wanted to invite all her friends and family, especially the Joy in the Morning Club, Little Tommy, Seymore, the Mexicans and Lynwood.

Myrtis had suggested they have it at the Baptist Church's fellowship hall, an idea everyone liked. She had even asked her preacher to stop by one afternoon to talk to the club about it.

After some cake and coffee, Grandma explained to the preacher that they would have thirty or forty people, including Little Tommy , who might take a bath, but probably wouldn't and Seymore, who might come as a woman or a man and might or might not be pregnant. Then there would be the ladies of the Joy in the Morning Club and

Lynwood who drove the church van, but really didn't have a church and actually worked at the Western Auto. Of course she would ask the Mexicans who would want to bring all their family and friends, including Jesus. Rufus Cole and Ben Cooper, she said, would be there, too, but would probably want to fox hunt first and not come inside until later...

The preacher squenched up his face and didn't even ponder the idea.

"No," he said, "no, that won't be possible. We only use the hall for church functions. Besides, I don't understand your connection to all these people. They should be with their own families at Christmas."

"They are my family, "replied Grandma. "But that's all right. I'll just have the party here at my house. We'll just make room. I won't let a bunch of Christians get in the way of Christmas."

The preacher finished his cake and said his goodbyes. Grandma motioned for me to come to the door.

"Look out the window and see where Ned is," she whispered.

I went to the kitchen window and spotted Ned right away in the bushes by the back porch. I relayed this information to Grandma.

"Good." That's all she said, "Good".

The preacher left and grandma watched quietly from the window. Then we heard the Ned's signature yelp followed by a scream.

"Good dog" Grandma said. "Good dog."

Grandma later said the prettiest lights she saw all Christmas were the preacher's tail lights leaving her driveway.

Elsie was dressed in her best star spangled banner outfit.

"She looks like she's just come from the Olympics," Grandma said. The women were going to the rental shack to invite the Mexicans to the Christmas party at Grandma's and Pearl had been practicing her Spanish.

"Just don't pull your pistol on them this time," Elsie instructed.

"Maybe you could learn to say 'stick 'em up' in Spanish," suggested Grandma.

For some strange reason, Myrtis Beane couldn't remember the pistol incident.

But before we went to the Mexicans' house, Elsie wanted to ride us all by her place.

"I've got something special to show you," she crowed.

As we rounded the curve to Elsie's, Grandma's eyes opened wide and her mouth fell open. There in the front yard was an eight-foot tall Statue of Liberty, complete with lighted torch and gilded crown. It sat on a brick foundation, surrounded by a flower bed ready for spring planting. I almost expected to see a harbor and ships passing by, but there was only Elsie's yard and, of course, her flag pole complete with American flag.

We were all speechless.

"Welcome to America," Elsie finally said proudly.

We rode over to the Mexican's house somewhat in shock.

"I fully expect to see the White House sitting in your front yard next," Grandma finally said, "and Ike and Mamie on the front porch."

Grandma knocked on the door of the Mexican's shack and Manuel opened it. Inside they could see eight or ten Hispanics sitting around a wood stove.

"Fleece Navy Dad," Pearl exclaimed, proud of her newly learned language. Three or four of the Mexicans leaped to their feet, a look of terror on their faces. They calmed some when they realized Myrtis was unarmed.

Manuel translated as Grandma told them all about the party. They seemed to be excited and promised to bring a chicken and rice dish "if they could find some chickens."

All the way home we discussed Elsie's statue of liberty. Myrtis couldn't seem to remember seeing it.

A week later Myrtis disappeared and her friends were frantic. They called Myrtis's son in Level Cross, but he had heard nothing from her either. Finally the highway patrol in South Carolina called. She had been found in Cheraw at a Gulf station when her car finally ran out of gas.

Myrtis Beane, aged 70, the victim of Alzheimer's.

"Go check the rabbit gums," Grandma told us, "I might make some rabbit stew for the Christmas party."

Willard and I squirmed.

"Just pop their little necks," said Grandma, making a chopping motion with her hand. "It'll kill 'em before they know what hit them."

Willard looked at me and I looked at Willard. Somehow it didn't seem like the Christmas spirit to be out killing rabbits on Christmas Eve. It was one thing to shoot them, but somehow popping their little necks didn't exactly appeal to us. And neither of us could recollect any tradition of holiday rabbit stew. We wondered why we couldn't just cook a turkey.

Willard and I went out into the fields grudgingly, our hearts not in the task at hand. But every gum was empty and the longer we looked the better we felt about the matter. Then we came to the last one and Willard frowned when he saw that the door had been sprung.

"Maybe it's a possum," he said hopefully, easing the door open. There inside was the skinniest, poorest rabbit we'd ever seen. Willard grabbed its front legs in one hand and its back legs in his other.

"Hit him," he instructed. The rabbit looked up at me wide eyed. He looked worse than death standing on a street corner.

"Let's take him to the house and let Grandma kill him," I said. "She's better at it. By the looks of him, maybe he'll die before we get there."

When we got back home, Grandma looked surprised to see Willard holding a live rabbit.

"That's the poorest excuse for a rabbit I've ever seen," she scowled. "He wouldn't even make a good soup. Take him back outside and let him go." She disappeared into a back bedroom.

About that time Willard must've eased up on his grip. Either that or the rabbit found new strength because he kicked free and for a second or two seemed suspended in the air. Then he hit the floor running and headed for the den.

"Did you get rid of that rabbit?" asked Grandma reappearing.

"Well...," answered Willard.

"Good," said Grandma, "you can help me make the punch. Go wash your hands first, though.

❧

Manuel and several other Mexicans knocked frantically on Grandma's door Christmas Eve, just as the party was starting. The little boy Jesus had disappeared into the darkness and no one had seen him for nearly half an hour. His mother was panicked.

Grandma listened to Manuel describe the situation, then turned to the Joy in the Morning members.

"We've lost Jesus," she told them, grabbing her coat.

"Well, I don't think we're that bad," replied Elsie. "We just drink a little wine now and then."

"We might have gone astray a bit," acknowledged Clovis, "but Pearl here's a saint. She goes to church six days a week."

"No, no, no," said Grandma. "The little Mexican boy Jesus is lost."

Grandma put on her coat and went out into the cold to help find him. Behind her followed Ned and two flea bitten dogs, black and grey, with patchwork faces looking much like they had been rolled in ashes. They were, evidently, friends of Ned he had invited to the party.

Grandma hadn't gone far when she spotted the nearby Baptist Church, parking lot full of cars, and all lit up for the Christmas Eve service.

"Don't these people ever stay at home?" she muttered, looking in a side door window. There she saw the small Mexican boy, sitting on the front row, intently watching a nativity scene play performed by the church membership.

Sitting beside him, arm around him, was Mrs. Dillard. Here, the story differs according to who is telling it.

What is known is that Grandma flung open the door and yelled back to Manuel and the rest of the search party and to anyone in general listening distance something similar to "Hallelujah, I have found Jesus."

Three elderly sisters on the back row immediately fainted and Mrs. Dohner's teeth were later found in the collection plate. About the time the choir broke out into song, Grandma grabbed Jesus from his seat and whisked him out the door into his mother's arms. At the same time, Ned and his two dog friends, not having eaten in several days, went after the flock of sheep in the nativity scene, who were played by several townspeople wearing sheepskin rugs. No one was seriously hurt, although three people did join the church that night and the local mortician threatened a lawsuit over his ruined suit pants, which Ned had mistaken for lamb chops.

Grandma at first claimed she had saved the boy from the Baptists. Later it was determined that he had entered the church on his own and that the Baptists had welcomed him with open arms.

We got back to Grandma's and the house was already filling up with people. Lynwood met us on the back porch and escorted us inside. As we walked in, I couldn't help but notice the empty peg where Jack Ledwell's fox hunting horn had hung. I punched Willard to show him it was missing but he was busy talking to Lynwood.

The party had began to pick up steam. Little Tommy arrived with his parents. We hardly recognized him at first, until Willard realized that he had bathed and washed his hair.

Lynwood was showing all of us a wrestling hold he had seen one of the Bulgarian Boys use on The Crusher a couple of weeks before at the wrestling match down at the school gym. Only he called it a "rasslin' holt" and said it was a death lock or something. He was sitting on the floor showing how the guy had taken The Crusher's foot and put it behind The Crusher's head.

"Like this," Lynwood said, straining to get his foot behind his head.

About that time Grandma called us into the kitchen. The Lilly family had made a surprise visit.

"Don't leave me like this," Lynwood cried. "My leg is stuck."

No one listened to him, though, as everyone made their way to the kitchen.

"We heard you were having a party," Mrs. Lilly was telling Grandma, "and just wanted to say 'Merry Christmas'."

"Well, isn't that sweet of you," smiled Grandma. "Watch the silverware," she whispered to Willard.

Mrs. Dillard and her husband appeared at the door with a bowl of collard greens. Mr. Dillard's pants were noticeably ripped in the back.

"We certainly appreciate you bringing these," Grandma told her. "I know how hard it is to fix collard greens. Here, try some of this chicken and rice Manuel brought. "

"I hope this isn't a chicken I know personally," said Mrs. Dillard.

"Did you know there was a pickup truck down in your pasture?" asked Mr. Dillard.

"Yes," said Grandma. "That's Ben Cooper and Rufus Cole. We let the hounds out and they're listening to them chase a fox. It's probably the same fox Jack used to let live in the rotted sawdust pile. Jack let him live there and, in turn, the fox let them chase him now and then."

"It looked like three men in the truck," Mrs. Dillard said.

"No," said Grandma, "It's just Ben and Rufus."

"I saw three, also," said Mr. Dillard. "You could see their outlines in the moonlight. Maybe they invited a friend."

Grandma stared out the window for a long time, her weak eyes trying to focus on the pasture. Then she nodded her head.

"It could be three," she said after awhile. "Yes, that would be just like them to get together to chase that fox, especially tonight. I just hope they don't try to plow tomorrow, after being up all night. And tomorrow being Christmas Day."

We heard a knock at the door. Grandma, warmed by the wine, didn't even peer out the window before opening the door. Besides, the house was full of people, one more couldn't hurt, she thought.

It was Sgt. Nelson.

"Mrs. Ledwell," he said sternly. "We've had a report of a kidnapping. A Myrtis Beane was removed from the Happy Hills Nursing Home early this afternoon by a man in a Baptist church van, some Hispanics, a mighty ugly bearded woman, a lady dressed in an American flag and a dog. I see that van parked outside. Are you holding this woman against her will?"

He looked inside, seeing the twelve Mexicans, Willard and I, Little Tommy with his new bandana, Seymore in his skirt, Nadine and Sam, Ned the dog, the Lillys, the Dillards and the ladies of the Joy in the Morning Club. Ned wagged his tail.

"Is this Mrs. Beane?" he asked, pointing at Myrtis. Grandma nodded.

"We just wanted her to have a Christmas with friends instead of being cooped up in that death house," said Grandma.

"Mrs. Beane," Sgt. Nelson said, "are you all right?"

Myrtis looked confused. "I think so," she said. "These people have been mighty nice to me."

"We were going to take her back after Christmas," Grandma said.

"Well, it's my nephew, Terry," Pearl Nelson said coming into the room and hugging Sgt. Nelson around the neck. His face turned slightly red. The Mexicans stirred uneasily when Pearl entered the room.

"Myrtis is our friend and a member of the Joy in the Morning Club," Pearl said. "We didn't kidnap her. We just didn't want her to miss our Christmas party."

"Oh," said Sgt. Nelson, scratching his head. "But the nursing home thinks she's been kidnapped. And her son is beside himself. I need to call them and let them know I've found her. I'll have to take her back, you know."

"Her son might be beside himself," Elsie grumbled, "but if he'd been beside Myrtis, we wouldn't have had to steal her."

"Could you let her stay until the party's over?" Grandma asked him. "It would mean a lot to us."

Sgt. Nelson looked over the people in the room and the piles of food on the counter.

"Only if I can stay with her," he agreed. "In a professional capacity, of course." He picked up a slice of fruit cake off a platter.

"I've made a coconut cake, too." Grandma announced. "Let's cut it."

The truth of the matter was that Grandma had first planned to make a blackberry wine cake, but had thought so much of the wine that she had drunk it and thrown the batter out the back door. So she was forced into making the coconut one.

Nadine began looking through the cabinet drawers for a knife. That's when she rediscovered the ants.

"Mama, there's thousands of ants in here. And what looks like a pack of molded weenies."

"I wondered what those little specks were in my cookies," Grandma said.

No one knows why a bird dog, one that wouldn't give a rabbit a second look outside where you could use a little help with the quickly burgeoning rabbit population, would care anything about a rabbit in a house. But Ned the dog had found the rabbit cowering under the Christmas tree, right beside the socks Grandma had wrapped up for Willard and me. For awhile, Ned figured only that the rabbit looking silhouette under the tree was just another present. But then the rabbit made the mistake of twitching its ears.

Ned let out a yelp and attacked the tree, successfully subduing it by pinning it to the floor while the rabbit watched bewilderedly from under the couch. Then, after Ned had become sufficiently covered with icicles and entangled in lights, the rabbit made his break for the kitchen.

But first he had to bypass Lynwood, who was still sitting in the middle of the floor with his leg stuck behind his head. Ned, now dragging the tree behind him, hurdled Lynwood in his haste to get to the bunny who had run between Elsie's legs. The tree, lights still plugged in, stuck on Lynwood, collapsed on top of him and allowed Ned to pull away.

Mrs. Dillard was the first person in the kitchen to spot the rabbit.

"Rat!" she yelled.

This set the crowd in the kitchen into motion. Mr. Dillard stood up just in time to be knocked off his feet by Ned, who plunged into the melee trailing a string of Christmas lights. Mr. Dillard's toupee, loosened earlier by the fracas at the church, popped off his head like a flying squirrel and landed squarely on the field of stars which partially covered Elsie's chest.

Elsie, hearing only "rat" and seeing the grey, hairy critter slide down her star spangled blouse, panicked.

Clawing at the blouse, she quickly came out of it, slinging it and the offending furry creature straight up in the air. The blouse fluttered down onto Sam's head and the toupee splashed into the punch.

Grandma said later that the punch was not harmed, it not having been spiked at the time.

The rabbit zipped under the table with Ned in hot pursuit. Mrs. Lilly, in her haste to escape what now seemed to be an infestation of rats, knocked over the table including the coconut cake and the collard greens. Grandma, seeing her antique cake plate along with a full bottle of wine heading for the floor did the only rational thing she could do and reached out and plucked the bottle of wine out of the air and cradled it safely in her arms. Mr. Lilly grabbed Mrs. Lilly, slipped in the collard greens, landing both of them flat on their backs on top of the cake.

In the confusion, Pearl Nelson's pocket book was knocked off the counter. When it landed in the middle of the crowd now lying on the floor, her .38 Special went off with a loud bang. This sent all the Mexicans scurrying outside. Some grabbed pieces of fruitcake before they left, probably to defend themselves with.

Sam and Sgt. Nelson, both veterans of World War II, hit the floor when the blank went off and the herd of Mexicans together with the rabbit and Ned trampled right over them.

But just as the rabbit made a right turn to escape Ned, Little Tommy reached down from where he was still seated and scooped up the bunny and held him close to his body. The rabbit, along with everyone in the room, suddenly became eerily calm. Tommy stroked him for awhile, then carried him outside and mercifully released him.

Ned, unperturbed, sat beside Mr. Lilly, licking the coconut cake off his shirt.

❦

With all the milling around no one missed Grandma for awhile. It was a freshly re-dressed Elsie who first noticed that she was gone. We began to search through the house until Pearl remembered that Grandma had said she was going out to the pond to talk to Jack.

"She's been depressed lately," Nadine mumbled putting on her coat.

"Yes," said Pearl, "she can't seem to get over Jack."

Several of us trooped out into the night to find her.

"I hope she's not going to do something dumb," said Sam under his breath.

We eventually found Grandma cold and shivering at the pond, standing near the water.

"Don't jump," yelled Sam.

"I'm not going to jump," said Grandma. "I can't even swim. Besides, it's cold."

"Momma, what are you doing out here?" asked Nadine. "You had us all worried sick. We thought you'd..."

"I just wanted to talk to Jack," she said. "I come out here when I need to talk to him. This is...was... his favorite fishing spot.

"Besides," she continued, "it was getting stuffy in the house."

"Momma," Nadine said kindly, "Daddy's not out here..."

"Oh, I know he's not," replied Grandma. "He's back in the house waiting to sing Christmas carols."

Sam and Nadine looked at each other like, well, of course he is, why didn't we think of that and he's probably sitting there with John Foster Dulles.

"I told him after that, it was time for him to go," continued Grandma. "He's had his party and he needs to move on. He doesn't need to hang around down here. We've all got lives to live. He said he'd wanted to go, but I wouldn't let him. So, I'm letting him. And it's all right."

We all just stood awhile and stared silently at Grandma. She was standing in front of a huge cedar tree. The moonlight reflecting off the wet branches made it look a little like it was covered by a million white lights. Then we all started back to the house at the same time, still no one saying anything. Grandma got in between Willard and me and put her arms around us.

"Oh, by the way," she said, "Jack told me to start feeding you boys something different, like maybe some fried chicken and gravy for a change."

After awhile, the party moved into the living room with Grandma playing Christmas carols on the piano and the Mexicans accompanying on guitars and maracas. We were all singing "Away in a Manger", our voices not exactly blending into harmony. It was more like a casserole of voices, with Ned the dog howling in the background and a faint scream coming from underneath the Christmas tree in the den.

That's when it hit me. This was what Christmas is all about: Different people, of different creeds and cultures and in Seymore's case, different genders, coming together as one to celebrate our Saviour's birth.

And we all knew if we could hear Ned barking we were safe, for Ned only barked at friends and family.

Never Look a Stamp Machine in the Mouth

Working in a post office can suck the Christmas spirit right out of an unsuspecting novice like a dog lapping up bone marrow. It has never ruined my Christmas spirit, mind you, but I've seen it stomp some peoples' flat as a ginger snap.

Christmases have a way of multiplying and magnifying themselves when you work with the public. Our customers are always right, of course, but sometimes they're so right you have to bite your tongue to keep from telling them so.

Take the Christmas we got the stamp machine, for instance. That Christmas stands out as one that almost removed the marrow from my bones. Stamp machines are wonderful contraptions, and if I had one or two more, I'd have to have additional clerical help.

I remember clearly the day when maintenance installed the said stamp machine and explained how this was going to put my office slap dab in the middle of the twentieth century. Just be careful, the technician said, and don't push this button. You hit that button, he laughed, and it will cause the machine to disgorge every stamp in that roll.

The stamp machine was an immediate hit with my customers, one in particular. I was back in the bathroom with my elbows knee deep in the commode cleaning it (small post offices don't have cleaning contractors) when I heard this voice at the counter.

"Sir," she said, "I can't quite figure out how to use your newfangled stamp machine."

This began the love affair between Mrs. McElroy and the stamp machine. Mrs. McElroy was a widow whose husband had gone to the great beyond thirty years before his time was up just to get away from her.

Everyone of us has a Mrs. McElroy. Mine was blessed with the ability to show up just before the clock struck closing time, usually with three packages to insure, a money order to buy and a letter to register to Taiwan. She would have everything she needed except boxes, tape, the addresses and money.

I suspected Mrs. McElroy to be on the beginning inclines of Alzheimer's Disease. She was also very poor, often wearing the same clothes many times in a row, clothes that no self-respecting moth was ever going to get near.

Mrs. McElroy never quite got the hang of the stamp machine. She would come in while I was still sorting mail and click her keys on the counter to get my attention.

"Sir," she would say, "could you change this dollar?"

Then she would go back out and drop a quarter into the machine.

"Sir, there's something wrong with this machine," she would yell and I'd have to convince her that stamps were 32 cents, not a quarter.

Soon, I'd hear another click, click, click of keys on the counter.

"Will these go out today?" she would ask, holding up two sweepstakes entries.

I would assure her that they would, that we didn't hold them until we got a bag full or anything like that, but two minutes later, Mrs. McElroy would be back, clicking her keys.

"What do I do with these three-cent stamps?" she would want to know. "I thought you said stamps were 32 cents."

The stamp machine only gave change in stamps. Being a good postmaster, I never told her what she could do with the three-cent stamps, but after awhile, my tongue had so many bite marks it looked like it had developed a rash.

But, back to Christmas. This particular Christmas, the stamp machine proved to be a big help, just as the technician had promised. I had only explained to Mrs. McElroy fortyleven times that if my window was open, I would be more than happy to sell her stamps. She did not have to come in to get change, go back outside and put the wrong change in the machine, come back in...oh, well, you get the picture.

But Mrs. McElroy seemed to enjoy her new found mechanical ability along with the exasperated look it brought to my face.

We had a saying around our office that we knew Christmas was over when Mrs. McElroy mailed her Christmas cards. One year she mailed them on Groundhog's Day. I asked her if she was just late, or getting a jump on next Christmas.

"I believe in Christmas miracles," she told me huffily. "I didn't have the money to mail them until now, but a little Christmas miracle has brought it my way."

I felt bad about my remark, but by the time the next Christmas rolled around I had forgotten it. That was the December 23 she came sliding into the parking lot against the curb so hard that her head bounced back and forth several seconds like a grey ping pong ball.

I looked at the clock as she gathered up what must have been a hundred Christmas cards and staggered into the outside lobby. It was five minutes after closing time and my window was locked tight. Her clock must have been slow, I thought as I watched her drop cards in the parking lot and then drop more as she picked those up. Finally she made it into the lobby.

"What do you need Mrs. McElroy?" I asked through the glass, rubbing my tongue gingerly. "I'm closed."

"I need some stamps to mail these cards," she answered. "Are you closed?"

"Yes ma'am, but I'll get you some stamps," I said.

"Well," she finally said agitatedly after what seemed like a half an hour, "I can't seem to find my money. I'll have to come back."

I don't know what possessed me to do it. Perhaps it was the thought of Mrs. McElroy mailing Christmas cards on Groundhog's Day. Perhaps it was refusing to let the season suck the spirit right out of me. But I unlocked the back of the stamp machine and pushed the button the technician had said never to push.

I heard Mrs. McElroy gasp as the machine spit out 103 stamps onto the floor. I knew exactly how many were on the roll because I had just inventoried my vending sales. I was reaching into my pocket to reimburse the stamp machine when she spoke again.

"It's a Christmas miracle," she exclaimed.

Then, in the same breath, I heard her say, "Will these cards go out tonight? And where are my three-cent stamps?"

Lost Looking for a Christmas Tree

It was not my idea to go out on Rocky River looking for a Christmas tree in the first place. But Hoyle thought it would be good for his New Jersey nephew Harold to see just where Christmas trees actually came from. Harold thought they sprouted in parking lots near trailers and strings of light bulbs, pre-cut and painted green.

That was why I was so mad when it became obvious that we were all lost in the deep woods of Chatham County. Well, at least some of us were lost.

If you've never been on Rocky River between Pittsboro and Goldston on an overcast winter day as the snow begins to fall you need to try it sometime. It will take you right back to 1750 when our forefathers first came down from Pennsylvania to settle this country.

There's not a sound to be heard in the woods except an occasional crow. Not a car motor, not an airplane, not even the reassuring civilized sound of a chainsaw.

One person alone probably wouldn't get lost out here. But three grown men and a boy, each one thinking the other was watching where they were going, is a doomed bunch to start with.

The day started off with little Harold grumbling that he was missing his cartoons and his M-TV, which didn't set too good with Willard and me. And then he began bragging about what he was getting for Christmas, some kind of Sega Saturn thing with 32 bits of power, 3D graphics and double speed CD-ROM, including Virtua Fighter, Columns and Power Rangers.

"When I was your age," said Willard, "I spent most of my time outside. Santa Claus brought us BB guns so we could shoot each other's eyes out."

"Yeah," I continued, tripping over a tree root, "that's why we're such good outdoorsmen. We didn't stay inside all the time glued to a TV set."

"Right," said Hoyle, "we didn't have TV back then. We didn't even have glue."

Willard elbowed me in the ribcage out of earshot of Hoyle.

"Kids," he whispered, "all they care about is what they get. They haven't got a clue about the real meaning of Christmas."

"Yeah," I agreed, shivering as the snow came down harder, "I bet they don't even know about Bowl Games."

I don't remember exactly when we discovered we were lost. It sort of seeped in on us gradually, like ice water into your boot.

Willard had found a nice cedar tree. Harold had wanted a Norwegian Fir, but Willard pointed out that, in the Piedmont, they only grew in parking lots. Harold pulled a little hatchet out of his backpack and chopped it down. We had voted to let Harold drag it back to the car for the experience of it, but when we started back to the car, none of us knew exactly where "back" was.

We huddled in a ravine out of the wind and discussed, among the three of us, just where we thought we were. I noted that I was getting mighty hungry. Hoyle said he was about dehydrated.

"You can go longer without food than you can water," he noted.

Willard said all he wanted was to be home for Christmas.

Finally Harold pulled on his uncle's jacket.

"I've got a canteen," he said, "and some food in my pack. I've even got some hot chocolate."

"Hot chocolate," Willard scoffed, "how can you have hot chocolate?"

"I've got some matches and a cooking kit and some packs of cocoa," he answered, pulling off his pack. "We can build a fire and heat the water and make hot chocolate, although," he added, "it's highly unusual for anyone to starve to death after only two hours in the woods."

While Harold built the fire, we munched on apples he had brought and tried to figure out where we were.

"I think we've been wandering around in circles," Harold finally said. "We've been by the old gnarled cedar three or four times already. I think the car's back that way," he said, pointing past the cedar.

We all looked at him with the skepticism adults innately have when it comes to any advice from children. Then we let him know that we knew exactly where we were, which was somewhere in the middle of Chatham County.

"Where'd you learn to build a fire, anyway?" asked Willard.

"The Boy Scouts," Harold answered. Willard gave him a look like "yeah, sure, they have Boy Scouts in New Jersey" when we heard a limb pop behind us. An old man stood at the top of the ravine.

"Do ya'll know whose land you're on?" he asked.

Willard admitted that we were lost, although he thought the car was somewhere just past that gnarled cedar.

"I figured ya'll were lost," the old man said, "when I saw ya'll go by the third time."

The old man graciously showed us the way out of the woods, which involved going straight past the gnarled cedar for about a hundred yards. And he only charged us forty dollars for the Christmas tree we'd cut down on his land. We all took turns dragging the tree, making sure Harold didn't strain himself.

That Christmas Willard gave little Harold a BB gun and Harold gave Willard a genuine Boy Scout compass complete with carrying case and instructions for its use.

Christian Nudists Bare All

Willard was worried about the emergence of the Christian nudist movement. Specifically, Willard wondered what these nudists would do for Christmas.

I told him I thought nudists were just like us, except that they went around naked, and that they probably celebrated Christmas just like we did. They just didn't get a whole lot of clothes for Christmas.

"What about the live nativity scenes?" Willard wanted to know. "I don't mind the baby Jesus being naked, and the camels are OK, too. But I don't know about the wisemen and the shepherds. And I can't imagine the Angel of the Lord without his bedsheet.

"Do they wrap their presents? And where do they hang their wreathes?

"And what about caroling?" Willard asked. "What if your momma pulled up in the driveway and the members of the United Nudist Church of America were in your front yard caroling? Naked. Nudism is supposed to be a family endeavor, but how would our families react?"

The family nudism movement reminded me of the family poolhall movement when I was growing up.

I can still remember the look on Momma's face when we told her someone was building a "family poolhall" in a neighboring town.

It was one of those incredulous looks, like "yeah, and I bet they're gonna have a family beer joint right next door."

Good Christian people just didn't go to poolhalls back then. They were dark, smoky dens of iniquity where all joints of vermin hung out, drinking beer and telling dirty jokes, leering out the door at the decent women-folk who passed by and sometimes when there was nothing else to do, shooting pool.

That's why the concept of a family poolhall was lost on Momma and why we wouldn't have wanted to go to one, anyway, even if Mom and Dad had packed us up and hauled us down there for a night of family fun. We didn't exactly want family fun. We wanted adventure.

But nowadays you can find Christian people everywhere. It's harder to find families, mind you, but Christians will show up just about anywhere.

I would have certainly loved to have seen the look on Momma's face when she read the news about the Christian nudists. I imagine it would have been one of those same "family poolhall looks".

Newspapers uncovered at least one Christian nudist conference that was held on the North Carolina coast not long ago. Christians are baring all for God, it seems.

"Christians can help make nudism wholesome, family oriented fun again," one of the organizers said.

By saying "again" this person hinted that nudism had once been family oriented fun, but had lost favor among the populace somewhere along the way. I searched my rather extensive memory, which contains many reminisces of family oriented fun, but could discover no family oriented nudism, only random instances of nakedness.

Willard could think of none, either, except the time we went swimming in grandpa's pond and someone stole our clothes.

I don't remember anyone coming to the Baptist church naked when I was growing up. Even though I'm over fifty, the age of no return, I think I would have remembered such an occasion.

Every now and then we would accidently happen upon a naked adult, which was such an unsettling event as to permanently scar us. But there were no organized groups meeting naked that I know of unless it one was of the adult Sunday School classes.

As a matter of fact, about the only family fun I can remember growing up involves going to the drive-in movie in pajamas or spending Saturday afternoons in Sear's Department Store. In both cases we were mostly clothed.

"We believe you can be a nudist and religious, too," another one of the organizers of this Christian Nudist Camp said. He, by the way, admitted to being a United Methodist, which may explain why I don't remember any nudist activities when I was growing up. Maybe the Methodists were doing it and we just didn't know it. That could explain why MYF was always more popular than BTU. And I always thought it was because the Methodists served food.

I don't argue with this theory that you can be religious and naked, too, but it just seems like the more naked people you add to the bunch, the more difficult it would be to keep your mind on your religion.

It would definitely change some of the religious services. The Lutherans, for instance, wouldn't be as anxious to stand up every few minutes as they are now. Catholics would spend more time kneeling, I'm sure. A lot of churches would be putting in cushions so their parishioners wouldn't stick to the pews.

One reason folks are deadset against public nudity is because it is usually associated with the original sin and most Christian denominations encourage modesty in dress so as not to inflame lustful passions.

I have seen some photos of some of these Christian nudists in the paper and, believe me, there is no danger of inflaming lustful passions. There is a danger of a mass exodus of people leaving to go into the monastery or to become life-long nuns, but not of inflaming passions.

These Christian nudists say that their practice is rooted in the very same Biblical teaching, such as the passage in Genesis in which Adam and Eve put on fig leaves only after they eat the forbidden fruit.

"We celebrate the body as God's creation," one nudist said.

Now, I know that the body is God's creation and I know He loves us everyone, but it's evident that He spent more time on some of us than others. Maybe there was a shortage of some parts at the factory and a surplus of others, but it is very obvious that not everyone was created equal.

I'd just as soon keep my clothes on, thank you. I don't even want to think about what would happen when the preacher told the congregation to turn the other cheek.

At least, as Willard said, you wouldn't have to worry about getting one of those ugly ties for Christmas.

Family Christmas Letters

We've all gotten them at Christmas, those colorful mass-produced "Family Christmas Letters" stuffed into our Christmas cards. They usually come from family we haven't seen all year long or friends we haven't seen in twenty years.

I suspect this started as a Northern tradition and slowly seeped South. No matter where these letters had their beginnings, it is evident that someone decided that it was too much trouble to write a personal note in every Christmas card they mailed.

This never was a problem in the South. We always wrote at least a note in each card. Sometimes we enclosed a personal letter. It didn't matter that we didn't know if the people we wrote were still living or not, we still wrote them. And we enclosed a picture of the dog or the car or even the new baby so everyone could keep up with the family.

Now we may get a photo, but it's a photo-Christmas card, with the entire family on the front, preferably taken in front of the Great Wall of China. It's stuffed into an oversized envelope to make room for the dreaded two or three page Family Christmas Letter.

And here's how it usually goes:

"If you haven't heard from us since the last Grubhead Family Christmas Letter (and you probably haven't unless you have E-mail or have been in the Far East lately) we're happy to report that we are alive and doing well. As a matter of fact, we are doing so well that all our stocks have doubled and Joe Bob has taken early retirement from his job as CEO of Microsoft at the ripe old age of 49. While at Microsoft, as many of you know, Joe Bob was personally responsible for developing not only Windows 95, but also Windows 98 through 2000. He still visits his best friend Bill Gates from time to time and they share old memories over an occasional bottle of 1672 French wine.

"Sally Sue, of course, is still active in various charities. Mother Theresa visited our palatial estate just before her death to consult with Sally over the plight of World Hunger. You may have read that Sally won the Nobel Peace Prize again for her work to ban land mines. They may as well retire that old Nobel to Sally as many times as she's won it.

"Little Joe Bob, Jr., as expected, has been accepted at Duke. As is Junior's history, he won't be just an ordinary freshman at the school. He has been handpicked by the Chancellor to teach trigonometry at the grad school level, a challenge he accepted readily. This will not interfere with his duties as Chairman of the Board of Exxon nor should it deter him from his cancer research. You basketball buffs know that Junior will be Coach K's starting center this year and has already been asked to try out for the L.A. Lakers. Naturally he wants to finish his education first, serve some time in the Peace Corps, solve America's drug problem and find a cure for AIDs.

"Sally Sue, Jr., is still special assistant to the Pope at the Vatican. You probably remember from a past Christmas letter that she graduated from Notre Dame in two days. She would have finished sooner if that old mono hadn't gotten her down. Those of you who know Sally, Jr., know that she hasn't let a little thing like having a heart transplant bother her and that she is not going to give in to mono. Of course, not everyone has performed their own heart transplant like Sally did at Johns

Hopkins in 1993. Her mother and father are so proud of her.

"This past year we vacationed, of all places, in the entire known world. You may have noticed the family photo of the Grubheads in front of the Great Wall of China. Joe Bob had several photo choices to choose from: the Pyramids, Bill Gates' living room, with the Clintons in the Rose Garden, playing a little pick up game with Dean and Michael. He felt the Great Wall photo, taken by his close friend Billy Graham, showed Sally Sue's face lift best.

"Next year the Grubhead Family Christmas Letter will be written from outer space, as Sally Sue has used her close relationship with John Glenn to wrangle us all a month long ride on the space shuttle. We expect the entire family to go along, although Joe Bob has had to break several commitments, including his golf outing at the Masters with Tiger and his speech "How I Personally Won The Gulf War For Norman" at the Pentagon.

"We miss you all and wish you a very merry Christmas and a happy holiday. Until we write again, you may reach us at Grubhead@aol.com. or in care of Ted Turner's ranch in Arizona."

It's my ambition to send out a Dixon Family Christmas Letter next year. I want to have the Dixon Family Photo taken in front of Central Prison in Raleigh if I can get the Dixon Family Car started. I just hope there's enough Dixon Family Cash to mail out all those letters.

Here's how my Christmas letter would go:

"This past year has been mighty good to the Dixon family. Little Jaybob was finally released from prison (see Christmas photo) where his usual talents stood out. He was named honor prisoner two years in a row and had advanced to head starcher in the prison laundry upon his parole.

"Warren has continued his duties as postmaster where he is continually in counseling for his nerve problems. He is so proud of his employees, many of whom have recently enrolled in the NRA's marksmanship program. He has asked Santa for a bullet proof vest this Christmas. During the last year he slept, ate, worked and occasionally mowed the yard. The highlight of his year was an outing to a movie where he ate some buttered popcorn. In his spare time he watched the Tarheels on TV and any other sporting event he could tune in, including tractor pulls and indoor soccer.

"Sandra completed another successful year as town clerk, a job we fondly describe as 'sitting on the town target'. During the year she answered such complaints as 'Why was my water bill 23 cents higher this month?', 'Why do I have to pay for water? I thought it was free.', 'Why didn't the garbage man pick up my husband's body?' and 'I pay taxes, why can't I have a junkyard in front of my house?'

"She has also cleaned house, mowed the yard and cooked one meal.

"Little Suzy Q. continued her winning ways at school by repeating the second grade, not once, but twice. Such consistency, not to mention perseverance, has always run in the Dixon family. She also created a commotion among the academic community this year with her science project, which consisted of lighting cherry bombs and flushing them down the toilets in the girls' bathroom at school.

"This year, once again, we did not get to take a vacation. Sandra did ride over to Wal-Mart one Saturday to buy some shoes and Warren read an article on Sacramento in The National Geographic.

"Our house, known locally as The Money Pit, continues to be our pride and joy and the talk of the neighborhood. So far, we have only had to re-paint it nine times.

"If you need to contact us during the year, please leave word down at Jethro's Garage and we'll call you back.

"We wish you all a very merry Christmas and a happy new year and promise to repay all of you who loaned us money during the past year as soon as possible."

Desecrating the Tree

A person's reputation, a bad one at least, follows them all their life. Make a couple of mistakes in judgment and you are branded forever. And a lifetime of good deeds can never overcome the notoriety of a minor shortcoming or two.

I say this because it came time once again to decorate the Christmas tree.

"You're not going to help with the Christmas tree this year are you?" Sandra asked.

"Maybe we just won't have one this year," she said hopefully, not even letting me answer.

"But what will we put the presents under?" I asked.

"We can put them under the bed. At least it's not going to fall on anyone."

A treeless Christmas sounded better and better until reality set in on us. Julie and Jamie, still too young to understand the stress, tension and potential for disaster of a Christmas tree, wanted one. It would not, they said, be Christmas without one. This was much like saying there could not be a Titanic without the iceberg.

So that's how Willard and I came to be appointed to go forth and find a tree.

"If we've got to have one," Sandra advised, "get a little one."

To find a Christmas tree you have to go to an Authorized Christmas Tree Place which, in this area, means any corner or vacant lot during the month of December. Willard and I found one easily, one that appeared, from the road at least, to have small trees, but rather large prices.

After several seconds of looking, we settled on a short, squatty, but quite wide at the bottom, tree that reminded Willard of his first wife.

"This tree has better hair, though," I told Willard, "and more of a personality."

"Enough of this reminiscing," Willard said as I loaded the tree in his car. "Did you mean to close the trunk lid on the top?"

"No," I admitted, "not really. But we'd have to cut the top out of it anyway to get the angel to fit, so it's just as well."

We got the tree home about night fall. I gathered the tree stand and necessary tools, including crowbar, chisel, chain saw, pliers, dynamite, WD-40 and Jaws of Life from the shed. Willard left on the pretext of "not wanting to see a grown man cry."

The tree went into the stand surprisingly well, with no 911 calls and no annoying screams that the neighbors have complained of in the past. It wasn't quite straight, but then it's a widely known fact that no tree grows absolutely straight. And with its low center of gravity, there was no way it could fall. If it did, at least it didn't have far to go.

I brought it into the house, set it in the corner and braced myself for the inevitable.

"That's the first tree we've ever had that we could put in front of the TV and still watch TV," Sandra finally said. "Actually, it reminds me of someone I used to know. What happened to its top?"

"Enough of this reminiscing," I said, "bring out the lights."

"Isn't this about the time you go out and get pizza?" Sandra wanted to know.

There is no earthly reason to test your Christmas lights before you put them on the tree, but we did. In doing so, I dropped an entire strand and bulbs went off like popcorn.

Finally, just as the last ornament was being placed on the tree, the moment came that we had all been waiting for. The tree fell.

"This reminds me of the kitchen light," Sandra noted.

Just because I once replaced a light bulb in the kitchen and the globe later fell into the sink, Sandra now thinks that I never bolt anything down or tighten anything sufficiently to hold it more than thirty seconds. Luckily with the globe, no one in our house ever goes near the kitchen, so no one was hurt. With the tree, we were all standing there to catch it.

We righted the tree and plugged in the lights and sat back to admire our creation. The lights glowed, popped and went out.

"A Griswald Christmas," Sandra said.

I took one strand of lights out and plugged them back in. They worked for about five minutes, then all went out except one light on each strand.

"Where are you going?" I asked Sandra as she left the room.

"To join the presents under the bed," she replied. "Where it's safe."

Sandra Claus and the Mattress

Sometimes Sandra and I decide on one gift for Christmas, something we both really need, and we agree that we will buy it for each other.

One year, Sandra decided we both needed a new mattress.

My ability to sleep anywhere, anytime, is well documented. As a matter of fact, by the time this story is finished, I will probably have completed several satisfying naps at the computer.

That's why I never would have dreamed that we needed a new mattress. We had just purchased a new mattress not many years before at the Mattress World and Bait Barn and I could not imagine that it had already given out. You would think if you paid a hundred dollars for something it would last. They just don't make things like they used to. And this mattress was a Surly Imposter-Pedic, which the salesman said is one of your top brands in Indonesia.

Sandra had noted that the said mattress was no longer quite as thick as our carpet. I suggested that we could sleep pretty well on the carpet and save ourselves another hundred, but Sandra didn't go for it. She wanted a king-sized mattress this time.

It seems that my tossing and turning at night had become an impediment to Sandra's sleeping, as well as some of the neighbors'. A king-size mattress would give me plenty of room to fidget and also give Sandra a safe, albeit small, space in which to sleep.

There seem to be several distinct stages in a person's slumber life. First you've got your crib, then probably bunk beds, next a single bed, the water bed and then maybe a double. Then follows the inevitable king and finally, separate bedrooms. I didn't mention the recliner because it is appropriate at any stage of life.

A king sized mattress was OK with me. I'm not a fan of the monarchy, but if it's good enough for the king, it's good enough for me. He doesn't look that much bigger than me, although admittedly I've never seen him in person.

The problem was, the Mattress World and Bait Barn had gone out of business. We would have to go to a real mattress dealer, one that didn't even carry the Indonesian Innerspring. I was worried that this mattress might cost us two hundred dollars before we were through.

Luckily I was wrong, as usual. You can't even buy a flat sheet for a king size bed for two hundred dollars. Then came another revelation. We would have to have another bed. For some reason, probably a marketing ploy, a king size mattress will not fit a standard bed frame. I had figured we could plop another mattress right on our old frame. It might poke out on the sides, but who would notice but us?

We visited several furniture stores. Double beds ran about $200. A queen-size bed will cost you about $300 and they'll even throw in a bottle of furniture polish. A king-sized bed? A cheap one will run you a thousand bucks.

We decided just to go for the mattress and steel frame until our ship comes in. Our ship, by the way, is mired knee deep in mud somewhere far, far from water.

We were fortunate that we had a friend in the furniture business because everywhere else we priced king-sized mattresses, they were going to cost us around $1,000.

But having a friend in the business paid off and we were able to buy a mattress for only $999.95. Having a mattress thicker than a pork chop has been quite a culture shock, though. We've gone from rolling out of bed onto the floor to having to have a step ladder to get out of bed. There's plenty of room on the bed, just nothing else in the room.

Then came other revelations: Not just any sheet will fit a king-sized bed, not even if you sew two of them together. The old comforter won't work, either. It looks like a postage stamp on the bed. And the pillows? They look like Barbie's and Ken's.

A comforter for a standard bed sells for $39.95 and you can find them anywhere, even in hardware stores. You can buy one for a queen-sized bed for $49.95. For a king-size bed, they start around $400 and these are the ones that feel like canvas tarpaulins and look like an old scout tent. And you have to special order them from Maurice's of Fifth Avenue. Does anyone know of a Comforter World and Bait Barn around nearby?

Everything worked out alright, though. We put the old bed in the girls' room. With the old burgundy and blue comforter on it, we will only have to change the curtains, put in new carpet, hang wall paper and re-paint the room.

The same goes for our bedroom. Does anyone know where we can find Tarpaulin Green paint?

At least if anyone needs a real night's sleep, we've still got the recliner.

Oh, Christmas Tree

From the Traditional German Carol "Auld Aggravaten Evergreenich Lightentangle" by Hemlich Maneuver, 1893.

Oh, Christmas Tree, Oh, Christmas Tree,
Symbol of Civility,
Your radiant branches hold the light
To honor that most holy night.

You're green all the summer long,
But just as soon as I get you home,
Brown needles fall onto my floor
As I drag you through the front door.

Oh, Christmas Tree, Oh, Cedar Tree,
I remember when you once were free,
But now with any kind of luck,
A Fraser Fir is forty bucks.

And what's more (and that's a fact)
You're probably forty-two forty with tax.
Oh Christmas Tree, Oh Bankruptcy,
My pocketbook is empty.

Oh Christmas Tree, Oh Christmas Tree,
Symbol of Gentility,
With rosin, bark and needles all,
Ground into my carpet hall.

And on the lot you stood so tall,
But in my home you only fall,
I've sawed and chopped, don't understand,
Why you won't fit in your darned old stand.

Oh Christmas Tree, Oh Death of Me,
Symbol of Futility.
So straight on the lot, then home you came,
Crooked as the Hunchback of Notre Dame.

I think that I will never see,
Such an ugly Christmas tree,
If only I thought I could,
I'd chop you into kindling wood.

Oh Christmas Tree, Oh Christmas Tree,
If you weren't already dead, I'd murder thee,
And hide your trunk in Dodson's Lake,
Then go buy a tree that's fake.

Explaining Christmas to Cheeto

I was wandering around the mall last Christmas like a deer caught in headlights when who should I run into but Alfredo Cheeto Mascara. You may remember my old friend Cheeto who visited me one Christmas several years ago from his home in Tibet. At that time Cheeto had stopped by on his way to Washington, D.C. to renew his country's sweet potato subsidy. According to Cheeto, the United States pays Tibet annually not to raise sweet potatoes.

"It's a good thing, too," Cheeto noted, "because they won't grow there anyway."

"We have a good deal," continued Cheeto. "We don't raise sweet potatoes and you don't sell yak milk."

Cheeto had become enthralled with our celebration of Christmas. I had taken him on his first trip to the mall where he had learned to fight for a parking place and how to give several different hand gestures. But just as he was getting acclimated to our way of life and had learned some valuable English phrases ("charge it", "it's not my fault", "don't shoot, you can have the money") the Bureau of Immigration had revoked his passport and sent him home. Cheeto's temporary visa had expired and he had been sent back to Tibet where he devoted much of his time to not raising sweet potatoes.

Well, it seems that the Bureau of Immigration had found that Cheeto's mother had been looking through a travel brochure of Yellowstone National Park while listening to a rendition of "America the Beautiful" on PBS when Cheeto was born. This automatically made not only

Cheeto, but his entire family and its herd of yaks, American citizens.

So here was Cheeto, new American citizen, back in America and hungry for knowledge of his new found country. Actually, it turned out that Cheeto was working at one of the stores in the mall.

"You can hardly speak English," I said. "How can you work in a retail store, especially during the busiest season of the year?"

"Easy," said Cheeto. "They teach me everything. How to run cash register. How to work microwave in break room. How to talk like a salesperson."

"How do you talk like a salesperson?" I asked.

"You say 'This is not my department'," Cheeto replied. "'It's time for my break'. Things like that."

I told Cheeto I was at the mall trying to do some Christmas shopping but wasn't having much luck finding anything.

"Just what is this Christmas, anyhow?" Cheeto wanted to know. "It sure has a lot of people upset."

"It's our most important holiday," I told him. "Don't you remember the Christmas you spent with us?"

"Yes," Cheeto answered, his face lighting up. "It reminded me of old Tibetan tradition called 'Civil War'."

Cheeto was still confused about our celebration of Christmas. On his way through town he'd seen several displays that piqued his interest.

"What do the plastic reindeers have to do with Christmas?" he wanted to know in his broken English.

"It's a long story," I replied. "If you think that's confusing, wait till Easter. We have these pink and blue biddies and dye Easter eggs and the Easter bunny hops down the Easter trail and leaves us chocolate."

"But tell me, did the Wisemen ride the reindeers?" Cheeto was persistent about this Christmas thing and refused to be distracted. "And how do the snow bunnies fit in?"

"Snow men," I corrected him. "Snow men."

"No snow women?" asked Cheeto.

"Very few," I answered. "The snow man business is mainly a male dominated field, although women have made some inroads recently."

"What is it with the reindeer with the red nose?" Cheeto wanted to know. "Too much eggnog?"

"He's the one who guides them as they fly through the night. The Wisemen rode camels," I told Cheeto, "but camels can't fly like reindeer. That's why Santa Claus uses reindeer."

Cheeto looked slightly puzzled.

"The Wisemen brought presents to the baby Jesus," I continued. "But no respectable kid wants to sit in the lap of a Wiseman. Their knees are too knobby. So we created Santa Claus to pass out presents. He's fat and jolly and most kids don't mind siting in his lap and having their pictures taken. The Wisemen were pretty photogenic, but they weren't soft like Santa."

"I didn't know reindeer could fly," said Cheeto.

"Well, they really can't," I admitted. "But Santa Claus is magical. Everything around him is magical. Besides, camels are too top heavy to fly. And Santa lives at the North Pole with all his elves, who make all the presents. The North Pole is the center of the gift industry. There's no commerce in the desert. The Wisemen didn't have elves to help them make all that stuff."

"Don't you think it's a little strange for Santa to live with all those elves?" Cheeto asked. "Grumpy, Larry and Moe and all the rest?"

"That's why we invented Mrs. Santa Claus," I told him, "to give Santa some stability."

"So, just because the Wisemen brought gifts to the Christ Child, you Americans have to give presents to each other?"

"Only if you want to save your marriage, your job, keep your family from disowning you and maintain your friendships," I admitted. "Not to mention warping your children for the rest of their lives. But other than that, it's a voluntary thing."

"OK, where do these snowmen come from?" Cheeto wanted to know. "I thought Jesus was born in a hot, arid climate."

"True," I acknowledged, "but we're always wishing for a white Christmas, just like the one we used to know."

"You used to know white Christmases?" asked Cheeto.

"Well, not really, not here in the South. But because we celebrate Christmas in the winter, it's natural for us to want snow. None of us, of course, could drive in it and it would cripple our economy because no one could get out and buy presents. None of us could get to grandma's house on Christmas day if it snowed, but we still want it. So the snowmen are an expression of this desire, no matter how deranged."

"Where did the Christmas tree come from?" Cheeto was full of questions.

"We used to cut them from the pasture and they were free, until someone realized you could buy them from street corner lots. We jumped at this opportunity to pay for them. The evergreen is a symbol. It's always green," I told him, "which reminds us of our money, which after Christmas, of course, is all gone."

"How about fruitcake?" asked Cheeto.

"Now, that one I can't explain," I confessed. "Some things you just have to take on faith."

"It still sounds a lot like our Civil War," Cheeto persisted.

"Christmas has nothing to do with war," I replied. "It's all about peace and love and giving. Christmas marks the birth of Jesus Christ and is the biggest holiday in the Christian world.

"We buy each other gifts, send cards, put up trees and decorate them lavishly. It is the one day a year we feed the hungry and homeless and in some parts of the country, people actually speak to strangers on the street.

"We go around to each others houses and sing Christmas carols. We visit nursing homes and bake cakes and cookies and take them to people we don't even know, including our neighbors.

"Christmas is so important that if it falls on a Sunday, churches usually cancel their services in honor of it.

"All this kindness stresses us out so badly that we are generally so beat down physically and mentally by the time Christmas gets here that we are actually glad when it's over.

" But it's wonderful fun," I added.

"Whew, no wonder everyone's so mad," said Cheeto, heading for the break room.

The ACLU and the Nativity Reindeer

A couple of years ago, the American Civil Liberties Union swooped down on Vienna, Virginia and again stood up for our Constitutional right not to celebrate Christmas.

It seems that there was a Nativity scene on town property in Vienna. A Nativity scene, of course, is the representation of the birth of Jesus, which everyone knows is the reason we celebrate Christmas anyway.

The ACLU, though, realized that our rights were in danger, so they took the town of Vienna to court and forced them to remove the Nativity scene. The town had thought it was safe because of a 1984 Supreme Court decision that found that a Nativity scene in Pawtucket, R.I., was permissible because it had consisted predominately of candy canes and plastic reindeer. In other words, if you can take the baby Jesus out of your Nativity scene, chances are you can appease the ACLU.

The Nativity scene in Vienna, in an attempt to ward off the Scrooges of the ACLU, was surrounded by two plastic Santas, one reindeer and one snowperson. The only touch missing was Charlie Brown in the manger.

A judge still ruled that the Nativity scene had to go, containing too much Christ for Christmas.

The next Christmas, the town of Vienna, still a little gun shy over this Christmas thing, ordered the Vienna Choral Society to ban any religious carols from its annual Christmas pageant and to stick to songs like "Frosty the Snowperson". The Choral Society quit the pageant rather than bow to the censorship.

Now Vienna has a Christmas-less pageant. But the ACLU still thinks that Vienna is violating the Constitution by having any kind of Christmas pageant at all.

The city of Morganton, N.C. got into similar trouble with a group called the Freedom From Religion Foundation. The FFRF asked Morganton to remove its Nativity scene located in front of the town hall. The Nativity scene was a 25-year tradition in Morganton.

I could tell by looking at the Morganton Nativity scene that it was, in fact, illegal. It showed Mary and Joseph, the Christ Child, an angel overlooking them and three wise men standing nearby. No snow people, no Rudolphs, no Grinches, just your everyday Nativity scene. It's a wonder the ACLU hadn't jumped on this years ago. We're probably lucky that the Freedom From Religion boys spotted it before it can spread.

Let's study this Christmas thing just a little bit and see what's going on here. It seems to me that Christmas, the real Christmas, came around 2,000 years ago, give or take a year here and there. This was a few years before Santa Claus, any elves or any candy canes came into existence. You may argue these points, but the fact remains that the great majority of Americans believe this.

When the first Europeans settled America, they brought the custom of celebrating Christmas with them. The holiday was here before there ever was a United States of America, or a Constitution. Christmas was declared a national holiday because it already was a national holiday. If the majority of your nation is taking it off anyway, you might as well make it legal.

This is a day on which all federal employees receive a paid holiday. All state workers receive a paid holiday. County, city, you name it, all government employees have a paid holiday for Christmas. The President takes the day off and even puts up a tree. I dare say that even the good ole boys down at the ACLU take a holiday.

The Postal Service even prints a stamp with Mary and the Christ Child on it. How brazen can you get?

It seems to me that it's time we ended this charade we've been playing and stand up and admit that we are a Christian nation and that we celebrate Christmas, not because Santa comes down the chimney that morning (even though he does) but because this is the day we choose to celebrate the birth of Christ.

If a government body, such as the town of Vienna or the city of Morganton, wishes to show the real reason it celebrates Christmas, a national holiday, who is hurt?

I say let them build their manger scenes and their stables and surround them with Joseph and Mary and the Baby Jesus and all the Wise Men that can be found.

If the ACLU wants to get involved, let them play the asses.

The Christmas Spray Nozzle

It must be particularly difficult to buy presents for a man because I sometimes get the weirdest stuff for Christmas. I don't know why people don't like to give money or gift certificates. Probably don't think they're creative enough.

So there's never any telling what will pop up under our Christmas tree. Sometimes Sandra Claus leaves me not what I want, but what she thinks I need.

It seemed like such a little thing at first. But when you are mechanically disadvantaged, you soon learn that small things are only small because most of their parts are missing.

I had grabbed the spray nozzle to clean out the sink the week of Christmas, only to have several of its plastic parts disintegrate in my hand.

After the shock had passed of realizing that the sink spray was no longer functioning, I was pleasantly surprised to find that no plumbing disaster had followed. There was no geyser, no leak, no drip, no puddling of water.

The spray nozzle had just broken and could certainly wait until a plumber arrived. And I knew, with our house's reputation, that a plumber was bound to stop by any day.

I mentioned to Sandra that the sink spray had broken. To the owner of an older home, this is just like saying the sun has risen one more time. You meet so many nice repair people when you own an older home.

Sandra has lived with me long enough to know my many shortcomings. My main philosophy is that if God had meant me to be an handyman, He would have given me some fingers instead of all these thumbs.

But just recently the whole family had gained a new respect for me when I had replaced a worn-out windshield wiper. They had lavished me with such praise and given me such royal treatment that I failed to tell them that the windshield wiper technician at the auto parts store had done it for me.

Now they thought I was Mr. Wizard.

We men never need anything for Christmas. If we see something we want, we buy it. And when asked what we want for Christmas, we just answer "Peace on earth". And we end up with a lot of swell coffee cups, flashlights and, of course, ties.

So I shouldn't have been surprised when the small gift wrapped package appeared under the tree that Christmas morning. It was a red cardboard and bubble wrapped replacement sink spray, complete with four-foot hose and at least 100 devious little parts. I could barely contain my excitement.

Sandra had found it at Wal-Mart and had purchased it because it said it was "easy to install." Plus, it was only ten bucks, much cheaper than your average plumber.

"And," she smiled, "you're so hard to buy for."

There are two basic laws of plumbing that the non-handyman needs to be aware of.

First, as my friend Leon Routh of Liberty Hardware says, "Never plumb at night."

And secondly, "To put the new part on, first the old part must come off."

Forced to show my hand--or my un-hand--I decided to install the sink spray. Remembering the treatment I had received when I returned triumphantly with the new windshield wiper, I figured a new sink spray would earn me several meals in front of the TV during the upcoming bowl games.

Here is the record of that ordeal:

Day One: Discover that Elastic Man could not get a wrench under the sink to unscrew the old spray hose. If he could, he would not be muscular enough to force it from its 200-year-old coupling. I even offer to pay Jamie, with her small hands, to try. She is unsuccessful.

I have found in my varied plumbing experiences that the old part rarely comes off. The entire plumbing system of the house however, and sometimes the neighborhood , will crumble around it.

Day Two: Purchase a basin wrench for $19.95. This is a wonderful tool and unscrews the hose in seconds. Since I will never again use this tool unless demoniacally possessed, I figure the cost at $5.00 a second, is still cheaper than a plumber.

Open package with new sink spray hose, spray head and collar. Many of the smaller parts fall into the sink and disappear down the drain. There seem to be enough parts remaining, however, to finish the job.

Assemble the spray head to collar using different combinations of O-rings, plastic spacers and metal clips. Eventually refer to directions. Directions say "Attach spray head to collar." Illustration, however, shows an apparatus similar to a nuclear power plant.

Spray head sprays fine, except it sprays out the back of the collar. Experiment with this for a few minutes and finally decide that Sandra may not see the added benefit of being able to wash her face while using said spray nozzle. Use knife to pry off metal clip and cut finger. Hunt down various parts that I have thrown around the kitchen to break the monotony and to release anxiety.

Reattach spray head. Now sprays out back and sides at same time. Notice that a few drips come out of the nozzle. Ponder this new development and can foresee how Sandra could wash both hands and curtains at same time.

Day Three: Return to Wal-Mart to purchase another replacement sink spray with four-foot hose. Cost: Ten more dollars, plus gas and time. Still cheaper than two plumbers and a steak dinner.

This time, miraculously, sink spray works right first time.

Leave instructions for no one to touch it.

Sandra says that electric iron has short in it, but someone has told her a new cord would be "easy to install".

Return to Wal-Mart and purchase two new irons. Take basin wrench and break old iron into 2,000 pieces.

Make note for next year: If asked what I want for Christmas, say a sweater.

Either that or plumber gift certificates.

The Christmas Party

To my knowledge, the only time Willard had ever been to the Country Club was when he and I got booted out for trespassing. That's why it was hard for me to believe he'd been invited to a party there.

But he had because he showed me the invitation.

Right there in black and white Old English twelve point intaglio on off-white unrecycled paper it said:

"You are invited to a Christmas party at the home of Dr. and Mrs. Edgar Fishbaum, 132 Elegant Acres Lane, at 8:00. Hors d'oeuvres will be served. RSVP."

"Willard," I said when I saw the invitation, "I don't mean to throw a damper on your holiday spirit, but I don't think this is meant for you."

"It was in my post office box," he replied. "Possession is nine-tenths of the law."

"Yeah, but who was it addressed to?"

Having worked many years for the Postal Service, I knew that mistakes could be made. Letters got in the wrong box. But people gave them back, they didn't open them and go to parties they weren't really invited to.

"It was addressed to me," Willard answered defensively.

I asked to see the envelope but Willard had thrown it away at the post office.

"When you call Mrs. Fishbaum, she'll set you straight," I told him. "And don't say I didn't tell you."

"Why do I have to call her?" he wanted to know.

"Because it says 'RSVP'," I said. "It's a French phrase that means 'parle vous Francis'. Translated, that means 'call me and let me know if you're coming'. But they want you to call them so they can tell you not to come."

"Looks like they'd just say what they mean," he said. "What's a horse duvers? More of that French gobbedlygook?"

"That's those little bitty sandwiches and crackers with Cheese Whiz and stuff like that," I told him. "You'd better eat twice before you go over there."

"Oh, yeah," said Willard, "like Penrose sausages and pickled eggs. A man could starve on stuff like that."

"You're not going to have to worry about that," I said. "You'll never get past the front door. As soon as Mrs. Fishbaum finds out you have an invitation to her party she'll cancel it and move somewhere far away. Either that or commit suicide."

Willard looked hurt.

But he called Mrs. Fishbaum from my house and after a few uneasy minutes on her part, she evidently decided that Dr. Fishbaum must have had a lapse in judgment and invited Willard. Because she thanked him for calling and told him she looked forward to seeing him at the party.

I reminded Willard that he hadn't been to the Country Club since we got caught trespassing there as kids. We had heard that we could make a few extra bucks by selling used golf balls to the pro-shop there. We just didn't know where to find these used golf balls until Willard had his brain storm: on the golf course, where else?

We picked a Saturday morning to go searching for the golf balls. The Country Club was a short walk through the woods from our homes and it just so happened that we popped out right on the ninth green. There were golf balls everywhere. It was golf ball heaven. Some had even stopped rolling. We gathered them up and went to the next fairway. There were more golf balls there. And people were friendly because a lot of them were waving at us.

Soon we spotted the golf course manager walking briskly towards us. I had that sudden feeling I get so often with Willard that we were doing something wrong and had been caught at it.

"Don't give him your real name," I advised Willard. Sure enough, the official looking guy wanted to know who we were.

"I'm Andy Ross," I told him.

"I'm Warren Dixon," said Willard.

"Well," he said later, "you said not to give my real name."

We were banned from the Country Club for life. They even took our golf balls and sent us packing back through the woods from whence we'd come.

But now Willard was going triumphantly back, through the main entrance at that, and most importantly he was going back legally, or at least semi-legally.

"Who are you going to take?" I asked him after the shock on my part had worn off.

"I guess I'll take Glory," he said. "She and I have been dating some lately."

Glory Hallelujah Albright was Willard's current flame. You must remember that this was before he had met Sue Lynn, but after he had been divorced from the lady wrestler.

"Good choice," I said. "She and Mrs. Fishbaum will enjoy discussing Glory's parole. And make sure she brings her own snuff. I don't think the Doc will be serving any."

I later heard through the grapevine that the Devines, Marvin and Jolene, received no invitation to the Fishbaum's annual Christmas bash. It was the first time they had been snubbed since Mr. Devine had hit it big in the chicken manure business. The Devines, by the way, had a post office box just below Willard's. I knew because I checked it out.

I never told Willard this because he was evidently looking more forward to the party than a frog gigging.

"I reckon I'll drive the Studebaker," Willard said one day as the party neared. He had started thinking about the logistics of the thing, I guessed.

"You could drive the pick-up," I said, "and Glory could sit in a rocking chair in the back."

"No, then I'd have to take the dog box out," replied Willard seriously. He'd evidently given the thing some thought.

"What are you gonna wear?" I wanted to know.

He said he thought he'd wear something festive but understated. Maybe his Carolina Tarheel sweatshirt.

"Well, do me a favor and don't talk to them about deer hunting, or dressing a deer, or deer burgers," I suggested. "People like that have better topics to talk about. Like the opera or Broadway plays. And they probably don't want to hear about Arnold Schwarzenegger, either."

"I'll just keep my mouth shut except when I'm eating those duvers things," promised Willard. Personally, I thought it was a wise move.

The night of the party I waited up expressly to see how Willard had done. I wasn't too optimistic, but then Willard was grown, well physically anyway, and I figured he could handle the letdown that would surely follow.

He came in around midnight.

"It was great," he announced. "I didn't even have to bring my own beer. They had beer right there. And they didn't mind the mud at all."

"Mud?" I asked.

"Yeah, me and Glory walked across the yard. We didn't know it'd just been re-seeded," Willard said.

"Turned out that Glory knew Mrs. Fishbaum," he continued. "They were in AA together. Glory showed everybody her tattoo. They'd never seen one *there* before. And me and Ed been sitting in his den for the last hour talking about deer hunting. I'd been deer hunting on his farm for years and didn't know it. He didn't know it, either."

"Who's Ed?" I asked.

"Ed Fishbaum," Willard said, like I was dumb or something. "He said he was sorry I had been left off the guest list in the past but he'd see to it that I was put back on permanently."

"Oh, yeah, Ed remembered you, too." related Willard. "He said you were the one who got caught stealing golf balls on the golf course when you were a kid. You and that Andy Ross guy."

Christmas Stress

A hot holiday topic is stress. It seems that Christmas, for one reason or another, brings more stress than your average holiday. I was reading an article recently on "Dodging Stress Through the Holidays" This is opposed to the ever popular "Jumping Right Straddle of Stress", which is more familiar to most of us.

It seems that a great deal of stress is caused by: 1. Adults having too much to do. 2. Children having too little to do.

This is a great concern to me. For instance, why is it that those adults among us who need the time the worst have so little of it? The month of December tends to run up on us like a speeding locomotive, yet to a child it comes like a slug stuck in glue.

The key here, of course, is to put the little tykes to work, so that time will pass like lightning for them, too. You must be warned, though, that unlike when you were growing up, there are now child labor laws, so you might want to check with a lawyer before you put Junior in the mines.

Another serious cause of holiday stress is the feeling that you must please everyone by finding the perfect gift. Part of this can be avoided by merely asking the person what they want for Christmas. You will have nieces and nephews who will not only tell you what they want and where to find it, but also how to finance it.

Then there are those who will say "Oh, you don't have to buy me anything." Don't fall for this. What they actually mean is "If you don't buy me something nice, you're out of the will, Buster."

Then there's the stress of not bothering to find the perfect gift. A good hint here is not to buy your wife's present at the hardware store. The local convenience store is another place to avoid, unless of course it's Christmas day and everything else is closed.

A good idea here is to begin shopping early. Hint: Christmas Eve is not early.

Let's say your niece has suggested that she might like a Liz Taylor limited edition commemorative Barbie, a doll you should be able to find in any self-respecting toy store with no trouble. You may wait until the last minute only to find that there were, at the most, three of these dolls made in the whole country and executives of the company bought these. So you end up buying "Potty Baby" instead. Believe me, you are in for a lot of stress.

Money causes much stress during Christmas. One way to combat this is to put away some money in a Christmas Club savings account every payday in order to be ready for Christmas. This way you would have about $29 saved by December and probably vault into another tax bracket because of the interest.

Or you could win the lottery, although if you're normal you probably don't have to worry about this. Have you ever noticed the kind of people who win the lottery? It's always these characters who say "No, I don't think Sadie and I will quit our jobs down at the chicken plant. We have grown to love de-beaking biddies. No, the money won't change us none. We might buy Momma a new doublewide, but mostly we'll just put the $40 million under the mattress."

There is a large amount of stress involved in finding a Christmas tree. Years ago you could just go out, chop down a tree and bring it home like the triumphant hunter-gather. You didn't have to worry about which lot to buy it from (the Christmas trees for the blind lot, the high school boosters club lot, or the guys from the mountains who sleep in the RV lot). You also didn't have to ponder which credit card to put it on or if you were overdrawn or not.

You didn't have to shake it to see if the needles fell out faster than the hair on your head or check to see if it had been spray painted green. And you didn't even have to put it in water because you put it up on Christmas Eve, not Labor Day.

Overeating can bring on much stress, not only to you but to those around you. On a good Christmas, you can eat six meals easily. This year, try eating only five. Or maybe you'll get lucky and Santa will bring you the Ronco Stomach Pump.

One way to avoid Christmas stress is to find some quiet time during the holidays. You really need to be committed to stop holiday stress.

Some institutions offer excellent accommodations. Just don't tell anyone where you've gone.

Shop 'till You Drop

I don't remember exactly when I realized there was a difference between men and women. Oh, I don't mean that difference. I mean a philosophical difference. An esoteric difference. A metaphysical difference. A shopping difference.

I bring this up only because we have entered the shopping season of the year. This is the Super Bowl of shopping. The Final Four. The Christmas season will make or break many retailers and they are out to whip us into a shopping frenzy.

I blame a lot of this on the Three Wise Men. They're the ones who started it all in the first place. Sandra doubts this story on the basis that there never has been one wise man, much less three.

Whatever the case, it's pretty well established that this frankincense and myrrh business led directly to Power Rangers, Snake Lights and the dreaded after Thanksgiving sales.

If you've never noticed this shopping difference in the sexes, go to the grocery store and watch men and women shop. Granted, this is provided you can find a man in a grocery store. A man will have a grocery list of a gallon of milk and a box of saltines. He will not take a cart. Then he wouldn't take a cart if he was going to buy 432 items, but that's another story.

The man will immediately go to the cracker aisle and before you can say "paper or plastic", he's on the way home. Of course, he's got the wrong kind of milk and crackers, but he's done it swiftly and efficiently.

The woman, however, will have her list of milk and crackers and will immediately grab a cart. Then she will begin browsing through the vegetables and proceed with much precision to go down each and every aisle, even the dogfood and baby goods aisles.

Sandra says this is because "there are things that aren't on the list" but I know that it's the innate and instinctive desire of women to shop till they drop.

In prehistoric days, the caveman went out with one goal in mind: to bring home the bacon. With this accomplished, he retired to his cave to wait for TV to be invented.

Nowadays, we men retain this "hunt it, find it and bring it home" philosophy. If Sandra is looking for a blue, short sleeve, V-necked blouse, I can go to it like a bird dog in a convey of quail. Then I'm ready to go home.

But to her the fun is in the hunt, not the kill. Even though I've found the exact one she's looking for, she contends that "we might find a cheaper, nicer, better made, higher priced one somewhere else".

On the Day After Thanksgiving, which is quickly becoming a separate holiday in itself, I figured that if everybody was going hunting at the same place, we should head for happier hunting grounds. But Sandra, Julie and Jamie were all of the opinion that we should go, of all places, to the mall.

"But that's where everyone else is going," I protested. "It's the most crowded place this side of Hong Kong."

But that's where they wanted to go, so I wished them Godspeed. This was the same trip I had participated in the year before and while I had survived it, my hip joints had begun to disintegrate after only 12 hours of shopping and were still recuperating.

And, as Miss Piggy once said, "When you are in love with someone you want to be near him all the time, except when you are out buying things and charging them to him."

They called me twice from their shopping spree, from two different cities and assured me they had enough provisions to hold out. I urged them to rent a motel room if they thought they couldn't get home by morning.

But they returned safe and sound, downplaying the crowds and claiming "there weren't as many people this year" which meant there was somewhat less ten zillion shoppers this time.

I think they now have enough Frequent Shopper Miles for a free trip to San Francisco. And they actually came home with a few Christmas presents, although they are fully aware that there is still three weeks till Christmas.

As Sandra says, whoever says money doesn't buy happiness didn't know where to shop.

The Week Before Christmas

It was a typical week before Christmas at our house.

We were supposed to go down to the local church and see the live nativity scene, but the event had been cancelled. Sandra said that some of the bags had fallen off the ponies and injured the shepherds.

"Bags on the ponies?" I asked.

"You don't think they had real camels, do you?" she replied.

Hoyle had heard that the Angel of the Lord had been smoking on top of the stable and set the hay on fire.

"They had to call the fire department," he said, "and everybody's beards fell off when they got wet."

Willard said it was cancelled because they couldn't find three wise men and a virgin.

So Hoyle and Willard had come over to our house anyway under the pretense of wanting to see our miracle Christmas tree, the one that was still standing after eight days.

Willard swore he could see the likeness of Sweet Baby James Taylor in the branches. Hoyle said the tree would likely become a shrine, drawing pilgrims from near and far. Sandra explained that it was merely a lapse of the laws of gravity that allowed the tree to stand and really nothing to get excited about.

I knew, of course, that it was nothing more than pure skill, honed and perfected over the years. I even harbored thoughts of starting a seasonal business, "Warren's Christmas Tree Installation" to take advantage of my talents.

Nevertheless, I stood near the tree to catch it in case Willard or Hoyle breathed too heavily.

Actually Willard and Hoyle had only come over to drink my eggnog and postpone the inevitable. They were going Christmas shopping after they left our house, which usually for them consists of going down to the Sportsman Center and discussing which fishing rod their wives would like.

Last year Hoyle's son Hobart had mailed a letter to Santa so big it took two stamps, but Hoyle had never seen what was in it. So Hobart ended up getting clothes and wasn't too happy about it. This year Hobart decided to make sure he got what he wanted so he had registered his choices at the House of Toys gift registry.

"Aren't computers wonderful?" Hoyle said. "We used to circle our choices in the Sears catalog, leave it open where everyone could see it and Santa still ignored it. Now kids can register their gifts by computer and Santa can ignore them electronically."

"Yeah," I said, "maybe we'll draw names electronically. Sandra's sister calls us and reads ours off to us now. Next year maybe we can get them by e-mail."

Willard and Sue Lynn had just gotten back from Myrtle Beach where they had seen the Rockette's Christmas Extravaganza. The Rockettes, Willard said, was the best Christmas show he'd ever seen.

"You must not have gone with us to see the Christmas Tractor Pull," I reminded him. "Now that was a sight to see. All those tractors decorated with blinking Christmas lights."

"Or the Christmas Catfish Stew", noted Hoyle. "Although I liked the Christmas Pig Picking better."

"Well, the Rockettes were absolutely uplifting," he gushed. "And they had five live camels on stage. Last year they only had three."

"Somehow that doesn't equate," I said.

"I know," said Willard. "There were only three Wise Men. I don't know why they had five camels."

"No," I replied, "the Rockettes and Christmas. How did they manage to combine the two?"

"For the Santa Claus scene they all wore little Santa suits," he said.

"What did they wear for the nativity scene?" I wanted to know.

"I honestly don't remember," said Willard. "But during the March of the Toy Soldiers, they were absolute precision. And there were midgets on stage portraying Santa's elves and live sheep and donkeys and taped music and everything. It was all professionally and beautifully done. It really put you in the spirit of Christmas to see it."

"Aren't you just saying that because there were all those pretty women dancers on stage kicking like crazy, all of them six-foot-seven and equally beautiful?"

"No," replied Willard, "it was really an inspiring Christmas show. It would have been a moving, stirring event even without all those dancers. As a matter of fact most of the time, I didn't even notice them.

"Pass me another D-cup of that leg-nog won't you?"

A Christmas Encyclopedia

A

Alpaca-the sweater your Aunt Norma knits for you that you mistake for a quilt.

Angels-what the kids become a week before Christmas.

Are-as in "Are you ready for Christmas"? You will hear this 900 times.

B

Bah- as in "Bah Humbug", typical seasonal greeting.

Bedford Falls-where Jimmy Stewart is from.

Bowl full of Jelly-your stomach, the day after Christmas. See also *"liposuction"*.

Bells-as in "I heard the bells on Christmas Day". Often caused by one too many eggnogs the night before. See also "H*angover*".

Boomerang Effect-send a Christmas card to someone, you'll get one back.

Blue Christmas-What you'll have if you buy your wife that Lava Lamp.

C

Carols-Tradition Christmas songs, such as "The Barking Dog Song" or "Grandma Got Run Over by a Reindeer".

Cash-once popular ancient gift; now obsolete.

Chia-as in "Chia Pet", good gift for mom.

Chipmunks-Famous singing group. See also "A*spirin*".

Clearance-as in "Clearance Sale", only held after you've purchased your gifts; also the distance between the top of the tree and the ceiling, often equal to one half the height of the angel decoration.

Counselors-what you'll need after it's all over.
Cards-as in "Plastic".

D

Debt-see also *"overcharged"*.
Day After Christmas Sales-see also "H*alf price*" and "B*roke*".

E

Evergreen-After three days, what your tree is not.
Eggnog- a popular drink found only during season. See also *"spiked"*.
Exchanging-as in "exchanging gifts". What you do the day after Christmas.

F

Fruitcake-what you are for thinking you'll get a Christmas bonus.
Frosty-see also *"mug"*.

G

Gift-see also "D*oesn't fit*". If you try to find the perfect one, see also "C*ounselor*".
Games-the reindeer played them.
Ghost-of Christmas yet to come: credit card bills.
Grandparents-relatives who buy your kids drums.

H

Handel-responsible for "Messiah", see also "T*hree hours of misery*".
Half price-what you could have bought those presents for if you'd waited until after Christmas.
"How still we see thee lie"- Dad on the couch Christmas night.

I

Icicles-long silver decorative strips found in the carpet behind furniture six months after Christmas.
Intoxicated-see also "E*ggnog*".
Irregular-The shirt size mother-in-law buys you. See also "F*ruitcake*"; also "L*axative*".

IOU-something you get from your brother-in-law.

It-as in "It only comes once a year", in this instance we are talking about eggnog.

It's-as in "It's A Wonderful Life", a popular Christmas movie; see also "*Run Into Ground*".

J

Jesus-often forgotten as the reason for the season.

K

Karo-as in syrup, used in pecan pies. See also "*Bowl full of jelly*".

L

Lights-things on the tree that go out when plugged in.

Liposuction-preferred method of losing weight after the holidays.

M

Mistletoe-dangerous, poisonous holiday plant. see also "*Black-eye*".

Martha-Martha Stewart, godmother of Christmas crafts; see also "*Justifiable Homicide*".

N

Necktie-perfect gift for Dad; see also "*Exchange*".

O

Overcharged-what the kids are on Christmas Eve.

Overdraft-Financial process which makes Christmas possible; familiar term to Christmas veterans.

Oxygen-what you'll need when the charge card bills start arriving.

One-as in One O'clock, the time you get to bed on Christmas morning.

P

Poinsetta-Christmas plant that if you set in dark after holidays will turn brown.

Plastic-see "*preferred methods of payment*".

Q

Quadruple-what you pay for gifts before Christmas.
Quaff-see also "*headache*".

R

Return-Department wife will take gifts you bought her.
Refund-Something you are not eligible for; you may, however, trade it for a different color.
Receipt-A slip of paper itemizing your purchases that the cashier throws in the trash can under the counter.

S

Some-as in "some assembly required"; see also "*Engineering degree*" or "*nervous breakdown*".
Shed-as "the tree is shedding"; or, "I can't get shed of Junior"; or "The rest of Junior's bicycle parts are in the shed where Santa left them."
Silent Night-the night the kids spent with grandma.
Socks-good gift idea for dad.

T

Tangled-see "*lights*"; also "*what a web we weave...*"
Tomorrow-the day everything goes on sale.
Two-as in Two o'clock in the morning, the time your children will get up.

U

Unrealistic-as in unrealistic expectations; see also "*Corvette*".

V

Visions-as in Visions of sugarplums; see also "*Overdrinking*".

W

What child is this?- Who knew the neighbor's kids were spending the night?
We Three Kings-good poker hand.
Wisemen-a thing of the past.
White Christmas-see "*Bad movies*".

Weather Radar-always spots Santa Claus around 7 p.m. so that kids can be in bed by midnight.

X

Xerox-what you do to those Christmas letters.

Y

Yes, Virginia-answer to the question: "Is there anywhere we can buy lottery tickets?"

You'd-as in You'd better be good, prerequisite for receiving presents.

Z

Zoo-What your house will resemble on Christmas Day.

Zero-amount of Christmas bonus you'll get.

Sounds and Smells of Christmas

Ah, it's that Christmas season again, you can tell by the sounds and the smells.

The smell of evergreens, eggnog and fruitcakes. A whole lot of fruitcakes. The smell of overheated radiators in the parking lots of the nation's malls. The smell of burning cookies in thousands of ovens all across the country.

And you can hear the sounds of Christmas in the aisles of the stores. The clattering of nerves, the gnashing of teeth, the whining of little children, the scraping of plastic cards across counters, the whirring of cash registers, the moaning and groaning of adults, the plop, plop, fizz, fizz.

They call it "holiday stress", as if it were just one of those festive maladies. But do you see a whole lot of people getting stressed out over Labor Day or the Fourth of July?

"Man, the Fourth of July has snuck up on me again. I haven't even bought the first fire cracker yet and Memorial Day has already come and gone."

"I bought my firecrackers right after the Fourth of July last year when they put them on sale. I like to shop early to avoid the crowds at South of the Border."

Let's just be honest and call it "Christmas Stress" because, frankly, no other holiday compares to it.

Professional counselors say that one reason Christmas is so stressful is that it is so sneaky.

For instance, you know for sure when the Fourth of July is going to be celebrated. And Labor Day is the first Monday in September. Valentine's Day is the 14th of February.

But Christmas always sneaks up on us.

Why is this?

One reason is that "Thanksgiving came late this year."

Let's see now. Christmas always comes on the 25th of December, but it sneaked up on us this year because Thanksgiving was late. Sounds like we might be going through a slight case of denial here.

We are a nation in denial. We should know right now that Christmas next year will be on December 25. But just as soon as the last ornament is stripped from the tree, we will again be in denial until next Thanksgiving.

"Can you believe Christmas will be here in (fill in the blank) weeks? I was eating a left over turkey leg and it was like somebody flashed a calendar in the reflection of the dressing. Where has the year gone?" (This is an obligatory rhetorical question, asked at least a dozen times by each person in the household.)

The few oddballs who actually accept the coming of next year's Christmas particularly grate on our nerves. You know, the ones who have already bought their cards for next year, have them addressed and are just waiting to mail them the day after Halloween. They're the same ones who, by the summer, have not only purchased all their presents at bargain prices, but also have them gift wrapped and ready to go.

These people are not normal.

I've always found that if we buy presents early, one of several things always happens: 1. The couple splits up and one moves to Singapore and the other to Egypt. 2. The person buys the same thing for himself before Christmas. 3. We decide we like the present ourselves and end up using it, therefore having to buy something else for the person. If we start shopping early enough, we can buy three or four things for a friend before Christmas and end up using everyone of them ourselves.

Another major reason for Christmas Stress is finances, or lack of them. The answer to this problem, obviously, is to use credit cards and plenty of them. You will never pay them off in your lifetime, but you have to leave your heirs something, right?

But the main reason for stress at Christmas is simple. It's Martha Stewart.

Martha Stewart epitomizes the high expectations everyone feels about Christmas when, in reality, your Christmas is always one of those Larry, Darrell and his other brother Darrell holidays.

If you watch Martha, you get this picture in your head of everyone sitting around the fire in ski sweaters, right there beside Michael Bolton and Barbra Streisand and the five hundred foot tall Christmas tree in the corner. Martha's telling everyone how to remove the stain from the hand woven table cloth she made while she's sewing everyone a scarf. The stain came from the wine she made to give to everyone in the known world. She also made all her own furniture, built her own 200-room house, knitted the carpet and created her own Christmas cards. And never burned a cookie in her life.

You, however, wake up one morning and realize the Christmas tree has fallen into the dog poop, the furnace has knocked off after blowing soot all over the entire house and those same flawed, imperfect people are waiting for you over at Momma's.

And they have no idea how to get the stain out.

I think we'll all need electric shock treatments before this is over.

And Martha should get the first one.

A Trip to Biltmore

It wasn't my idea to go to the Biltmore Estate in Asheville, N.C. Sue Lynn, Willard's wife, had suggested it. She'd seen an article on it in some magazine while she was waiting in line at the grocery store.

Willard did anything Sue Lynn asked. If she'd wanted to go to Kuwait, Willard would have been on the phone trying to rent a camel. As a matter of fact, Hoyle and I figured he was so hen-pecked that he had little red marks all over his head like chigger bites.

"Willard," I told him, "I've been to Biltmore and it's a big mistake. Biltmore is the largest private residence in the entire nation. It's got 250 rooms, 40 some bathrooms and just one man lived in it. When Sue Lynn gets home and sees her house, she's gonna think she's been robbed.

"I took Sandra one year and she hasn't been right since. Had to have new carpet. Even bought an electric can opener."

"If Sue Lynn wants to go, I'm gonna take her," said Willard. "You and Sandra are welcome to come along."

I knew there was no use wasting my breath on Willard. It had gotten so bad that Sue Lynn didn't even let his coon dogs in the house anymore and made Willard shave daily, even on Saturday. And there was no more cooking pintos on the kerosene heater, either.

Sue Lynn had about sucked the life out of Willard.

We picked a Saturday in December to go to Asheville. Biltmore was all decked out for Christmas and

Sandra and Sue Lynn were excited about getting some decorating ideas.

The girls immediately hopped in the back of Willard's Studebaker. I mentioned to Willard that we would have a safer trip that way, the women being able to drive better from the back seat.

I soon realized why Sue Lynn jumped in the back seat so fast. My bucket seat was rocking back and forth so badly that I had to hold onto the door to keep from lurching into the windshield.

"What's wrong with this seat?" I asked Willard.

"Nothing," said Willard. "It's just not bolted down. I was putting in bucket seats and didn't get through. Yours is sitting on cinder blocks."

Every time Willard slowed down I had to hang on so that my head didn't embed in the dashboard.

We hadn't gotten far when Willard asked me to look back and see if the Studebaker was smoking.

"No," I assured him. "It's OK."

Willard quickly pulled over to the side of the road and cut the car off.

"What's wrong?" I asked. "I said it's not smoking."

"Yeah," said Willard, "it's not smoking. That means it's out of oil." He opened the trunk where he had a case of motor oil, added a few quarts and got back into the car again.

"Let me know when it stops smoking again," he said.

I felt a little better about Willard after the bucket seat and oil incidents. Maybe I had been worrying need-lessly.

We got to Biltmore in fine shape, about nine quarts of oil later and immediately set out to tour the mansion. As we trooped up and down narrow stair cases to room after room after room, I began to see the fear on Willard's face.

"There's a Christmas tree in every room," he whispered to me once.

"Two in some," I replied. "And look at all these antiques."

We finished up at the indoor pool and indoor bowling alley. There were Christmas trees there, too.

When we got outside, the faces of Sandra and Sue Lynn were absolutely glowing.

"I can't wait to get home," said Sue Lynn. "I'm going to put a Christmas tree in every room. And we need to stop and get material to make some wreathes."

"And candles, too," said Sandra. "And did you see that paneling in the game room?"

On the way back, Sue Lynn just had to stop and see "The World's Largest Doublewide". I think she would have bought it had it been furnished with red shag carpet.

We got home and Willard was ecstatic. His Studebaker had only used 18 quarts of oil.

"I think this car keeps getting better and better," he marveled.

I asked him if he wanted to come over and watch a ball game on the tube. He couldn't. He and Sue Lynn had to rearrange the furniture, then go look at new paneling. I privately wondered if he didn't have to shave, too.

I started to tell Willard "I told you so" but I was too busy. Sandra wanted to go find a Christmas tree for the bathroom.

The Christmas Countdown

The Christmas countdown has begun.

I can always tell when Christmas is officially on the way. My friends Walt and Susan have finally finished decorating their house, known locally as Biltmore East.

This process starts around late summer and continues full bore until the last week before Christmas. During this time Walt hires professional guides to find many of the Christmas decorations which are stored in the far reaches of his attic. If that attic floor ever collapses, we'll have a bigger disaster than the California mud slides.

Susan's latest project is a two-ton Christmas centerpiece, something akin to the Space Shuttle, atop the dining room table, which OSHA has already condemned as unsafe. Walter was busy bracing the table and probably underpinning the dining room floor, too, before the holidays get going full speed.

Since it's obvious that Christmas is unavoidably on the way, there are numerous things you need to be doing and doing right now. I have itemized a list of things to begin working on immediately that will not only help you enjoy Christmas more but will also prevent you from the embarrassment of killing your in-laws.

WEEK FOUR:

Gather all your favorite holiday recipes. Pile them in the fireplace, light them and burn them beyond recognition. Be especially certain to fully destroy anything by Martha Stewart and Julia Child.

Go to the bookstore and buy a copy of "How to Overcome the Despair of Debt".

Attempt to obtain a home equity loan.

Call Mr. Cash.

Make sure all credit cards are current.

Write a Christmas gift list including everyone you will buy presents for and attach a dollar amount for each person. Add the amounts and total the list. Remember that "it's the thought that counts". Keep the list, though, to prove you were thinking about them.

Order catalog gifts.

WEEK THREE

Return catalog gifts for right size, color, etc.

Make a shopping list for the ingredients you'll need for your holiday baking. Don't forget the rum for the rum cake.

Draw names for the family gift exchange. Mark slips of paper so that you get "good names".

Take unfinished crocheted gift items you have been working on all year and place them in your rag bag.

Write a Christmas letter to include in with your Christmas cards and photocopy ten thousand copies. Be sure to write every boring detail of your year including the fact that the kids were accepted at Harvard.

Hunt for the Christmas cards you bought on sale last January.

WEEK TWO:

Start your decorating. If you're going to place lights on an outdoor tree, make sure you don't put many on it so that the tree looks deformed when lit.

Begin untangling lights. Test lights once untangled. Go buy more lights.

Send back catalog gifts again for right size, color, etc.

Have kids make creative, colorful gift tags, Christmas cards, decorative wrapping paper from tissue paper, construction paper and brown paper bags. Note:

These are usually so ugly that the kids won't even use them, but it keeps them out of your hair a few hours.

Mail Christmas cards. Make sure you have enough postage to include two-pound Christmas letter you've enclosed.

Assemble baking ingredients and rum. Throw ingredients away. Drink rum.

Give up finding Holiday Barbee and Tickle Me Elmo. Purchase Everyday Barbee and Tickle My Elbow instead. Hope kids won't know the difference.

Remember, it's the thought that counts.

Be sure you have plenty of film to capture the magic on their faces.

WEEK ONE:

Relax and enjoy the holidays. You're not prepared by any means, but neither is anyone else.

The Christmas Cabin

Good friend Willard and I went out, with his nephew Stephen,
When the snow lay round about, deep and crisp and even.

There was one thing that was absolutely clear to us about Christmas: That it was a magical time, a time when wonderful, unexplainable events often occurred. We never really understood why they happened, but we accepted them as a part of Christmas.

It was just to be a short hunting trip to show Willard's nephew Stephen what hunting was all about. Hunting used to be a part of life in the South, but had fallen on hard times lately with the animal rights movement, the building up of the suburbs and the disappearance of the forests.

Stephen had never been hunting, a fact that Willard thought to be cruel and unusual for a boy of his age and something that he planned on changing as soon as possible.

There had been a time in Willard's life when nothing but a Carolina basketball game would have come between him and a hunting trip, but that had changed since he had married Sue Lynn. Now it seemed that he didn't have time for anything important anymore.

Willard had gotten permission from his uncle to hunt on his land. Getting permission was one thing that showed Willard had changed since his marriage. When we were growing up, our creed was "This land is your land, this land is my land", a motto that got us into a infinite amount of trouble.

But, as Willard used to say, "if we didn't do any-thing, we wouldn't have anything to talk about."

We were going to have wonderful fun, Willard said. Just like old times. His uncle had told him that there were hundreds of acres for us to roam on and there were even some abandoned wells on the property.

"And," Willard had added gleefully, "there might be a squatter living in an old cabin on my uncle's property."

His uncle had gotten wind of the man from a deer hunter, but hadn't had time to check out the story. If he was living there, Willard said, his uncle was going to get the sheriff to remove him from the property as soon as possible.

"I figure," said Willard, "if we see him we can get rid of him ourselves."

"This 'we' you keep talking about," I replied. "That doesn't include me does it? I'm allergic to abandoned wells."

"Yeah, you and Hoyle," he said. "I wouldn't leave ya'll out of the fun."

So, that's how we ended up hunting with Willard and Stephen on Christmas Eve. We were to hunt a few hours, then come back to town so Willard could do some last minute Christmas shopping. Willard considered shopping on Christmas Eve "early".

"Christmas Day is late," he said.

We stopped by his uncle's house on the way.

"Ya'll be careful if you go near that old house down by the creek," he told us. "I don't know if that bum is still there or not, but I've been missing some stuff lately and I got a feeling he's been stealing it. And pay attention to where you're going. There's some mighty thick woods out there."

As we were hunting, none of us noticed the sky getting darker and darker. We were deep in the woods, which are dark enough in December, so it didn't dawn on us for awhile that we were in for a blizzard.

Stephen had killed several squirrels and we were all enjoying being in the great out of doors that the time sort of slipped away from us. That's when it began snowing fast and furiously, little stinging bits of snow driven by a north wind.

"Where'd this come from?" I asked Willard.

"We should have known it was gonna snow," he grumbled. "The weatherman hasn't been calling for it."

We decided to get back to the car as soon as possible.

"I don't want to catch hypothermia," said Willard.

"This reminds me of that movie where the plane went down in the Andes and everyone resorted to cannibalism," said Hoyle.

"It hasn't been snowing but fifteen minutes," I reminded them.

But we couldn't find the way back to the car. It's strange how snow will change the nature of the landscape. Willard admitted never having been on his uncle's land before and not having a clue where we were. I told him it was strangely similar to the time we had been looking for the Christmas tree down on Rocky River and gotten lost. And the snow was covering our tracks faster than we could make them.

Finally we took shelter in a stand of big pines and assessed the situation. We all agreed we were lost and it was getting dark quickly.

"We'll just have to stay here until it quits snowing," I said.

Hoyle noted that the guys in the Andes had finally walked out, but not before they had cut their buddies up into steaks.

As night came to the forest, the snow seemed to intensify. It began to be evident to us that we were stuck in the woods until morning, with not much shelter and no matches to build a fire. But when it got dark, we could see a faint light far through the woods to our right.

"Maybe that's your uncle's house," I told Willard. "Do you think we're that close?"

We figured it was worth a try, and all four of us walked into the wind toward the glow in the distance. That's when Willard fell into the creek.

"Well!" he hollered. "I'm in a well!"

"It's just the creek," said Hoyle. "I'm in it, too. It's up over my boots."

"Frostbite," moaned Willard. "We'll lose our toes, I just know we will."

"There's a house over there," said Stephen. We all looked across the creek and saw an old frame house through the snow, with a tin roof and smoke coming out the chimney, light from the fire place showing through a window.

"That must be the old house that bum was living in," said Willard. "Let's go."

We followed Willard to the house. The snow was two feet deep in drifts by this time and Stephen was having trouble walking in it. We got to the porch and Willard knocked loudly on the door. There was a stirring inside, but no one came to the door.

"We've been hunting," yelled Willard, "and we've gotten lost. We're freezing to death out here.

" And we've got some squirrels," he added.

The door cracked slowly open. A large, dirty, bearded man peered out into the darkness, looking warily at us.

"You've got squirrels?" he finally asked. We nodded and he let us in.

Once inside, Willard didn't dare mention the fact that the old man was trespassing and he, in turn, didn't ask us how we managed to get lost. He took our squirrels, skinned them, and put them over the fire in the fire place to roast. Hoyle, Stephen and I didn't try the roasted squirrel, but Willard and the old man did, eating heartily.

Aren't ya'll afraid you'll starve?" asked Willard.

"We've waiting for you to go to sleep," said Hoyle. "Remember the Andes."

Willard made a face.

"The old man reminds me of Santa Claus," whispered Hoyle.

"Yeah," said Willard, "but he smells more like his reindeer."

We explained to the old man that we needed to spend the night, but that just as soon as it got light, we were leaving to find our way back to the car. We didn't relish spending Christmas Eve lost in the woods, but didn't seem to have a choice.

"You're welcome in my home for as long as you need to stay," the old man answered. "I'm glad to have visitors."

We looked around the small cabin. There was no furniture, save a wooden crate the old man was sitting on. In one corner was a heap of rags and beside the fireplace was a pile of dead wood he'd scavenged from the forest. It was evidently a harsh existence.

But in one corner away from the fireplace I could see a small cedar tree sitting in a bucket in the shadows. It had been decorated with what looked like bits of cigarette packs and pieces of ribbon. Under it were a couple of presents wrapped in tinfoil.

"Ya'll ever been lost before?" the old man asked.

"Oh, yeah," I answered. "We're getting to be experts at it."

"Your families will probably come looking for you, won't they?" he wondered.

"Not until morning," said Hoyle. "Not in this blizzard. The only people out in this stuff will be fools and Santa Claus."

What we didn't realize at the time was that all the phone lines were down and the power had gone out all over the Piedmont due to the storm. Our families, though worried, hoped that we were spending the night with Willard's uncle. None of them had a clue that we were spending the night with a recluse.

"Ya'll will miss Santa Claus tomorrow morning," the old man continued.

"We'll get there in time," said Willard. "We wouldn't miss that."

"I don't believe in Santa Claus" said Stephen.

"Humph," the old man spat. "That's easy to say. You don't have to believe in Santa Claus. He comes whether you believe in him or not."

"I'm too old to believe in him," said Stephen.

"Not me," said Willard. "I'll always believe in him."

"Yeah," said Hoyle, "But you still believe in the Easter Bunny."

"Folks who believe in Santa Claus understand the good that lives in everybody," the old man said, rubbing his beard. "You don't always see that, either, but it's there."

We all sat in a circle, mesmerized by the fire.

"I bet you don't believe in angels, either," the old man asked Stephen. " Have you ever heard the angels sing?"

"No," admitted Stephen.

"Well, you weren't listening," he replied. "Just because you can't see something, is no sign it's not there. You have to believe in the magic in life..."

"Holy Santa Claus!" said Willard, standing up slapping his hand to his head. "I didn't get a chance to go by Wal-Mart and get Sue Lynn that watch. I was going to buy it this afternoon and slip it under the tree. Now all she's got is some underwear, deodorant and a steam iron."

"Can I have your chainsaw?" asked Hoyle. "I mean before Sue Lynn has your estate sale?"

"Oh, man," moaned Willard, "I am definitely in trouble."

There's something about sitting in front of a fireplace, watching the fire pop and crack, that sends you back to the dawn of time. You begin to see things in the fire that you're not sure are there, hypnotized by the flames.

After awhile, we all dozed off, curled up on the floor in front of the fire. I awoke during the night shivering and the fire had gone out. I threw a couple of logs on the fire and it blazed up. I noticed the old man was nowhere to be seen. I looked out a window and saw that it had quit snowing. And just before I went back to sleep, my gaze caught the tree. I noticed the two presents were gone.

The next morning we got back to the car and all our families were waiting for us at Willard's uncle's. Everyone had been frantic, except Sue Lynn who was used to such calamities.

We'd all agreed not to tell anyone of the old man, at least until after Christmas. That was the least we could do for his hospitality.

That afternoon Willard called me.

"Guess what?" he asked.

"We're going hunting again," I guessed.

"No," he said seriously. "That watch I was going to buy Sue Lynn. It was under the tree. The very same watch. It just appeared out of the blue. She was tickled to death with it.

"But I didn't get to buy it," he added nervously.

"Sue Lynn probably went out and bought it for herself," I told him. "She knew that was the only way she was going to get it. Either that or Hoyle sneaked it in to play a joke on you."

"No," he replied, "Sue Lynn saw it this morning before we got home. It was wrapped in tinfoil."

We told Willard's uncle that we had never seen the old derelict who was supposed to be living in the cabin. He later went down there and could find no sign of him.

It wasn't until months later that we found out Stephen had gotten a present that Christmas day, also. It was a book on angels and appeared under the tree sometime Christmas Eve, gift wrapped in tinfoil and smelling strangely of wood smoke.

The Wise Men's Wives

There's a lot of talk about the Wise Men and how they traipsed across the desert for the longest time following the star in the east that eventually led them to the Christ Child.

But no one ever mentions the wives of the Wise Men and the story of how they stood by their men on the eve of that very first Christmas.

There are several differences of opinion on this story, for scholars seldom agree on the exact way history unfolded. There is a rather large contingent of historians who don't think the Wise Men even had wives. The rationale here is that if the Wise Men were married, they would not have been called "Wise Men".

And then there's a group, Sandra included, who believes the word "Wise Men" is a contradiction in terms, much like "government intelligence".

Since there is not much written history of the Wise Men's adventure, let's imagine for a moment the scene that unfolded in the days before the Wise Men's departure.

First of all, it has to be remembered that the Wise Men decided to go off to the east without taking their wives. This must've have been a near fatal mistake.

"Er, honey, me and the guys are going off for a few days. There's a star in the east we want to follow. Do I have any clean underwear?"

"Oh, right, Leroy, you think you're going off with those other two goof heads who call themselves Wise Men? Aren't they the same ones I caught you playing poker with down at Hadijeh's Oasis? And what's so special about this star?"

This scene was undoubtedly repeated in the other two mud huts.

"You men are always going off to 'follow some star'. What about us? We don't ever get to go anywhere. We haven't been to the beach in years. I'll give you a star...

"And you think you're going to take all the gold? I don't think so. How am I supposed to buy groceries? Where's the kids lunch money coming from? Why don't you take the charge card and leave me the gold? I can't believe I'm sitting here without a thing to wear and you want to go off down east with the gold.

"What about your job? Do you think they'll keep you on down at the Used Camel Lot? The way unemployment is? Do you know how hard jobs are to find in the desert?

"Speaking of camels, we need a new one. Our's is on its last leg. That old one-humper is an antique anyway. How long do you think it would hold up on a trip?

"How long are you going to be gone following this star? What do you mean you don't know? I bet you don't even have a map. And I know you won't stop and ask directions.

"You need to start doing some things around the hut instead of planning these fool trips. The garbage hasn't even been taken out. And the sand needs mowing right now.

"I remember when Melvin next door left 'to get some goat feed' and never came back. His poor wife is on food stamps now. And you expect me to believe you're going 'to follow a star'?

"And that Darius is up to no good. If he's a Wise Man, I'm a brain surgeon. All he does is sit around and look at the sky through that telescope. I'm not so sure he doesn't have that thing aimed at that hussie's hut across the street. She walks around all the time without her sheet on and never closes her blinds.

"And what are you planning to do with that frankincense? You never wear that stuff around me. Are you seeing someone else?"

We all know the rest of the story. The wives relented, washed the Wise Men a few pairs of socks, ironed their robes, packed them a nice lunch and sent them on their way. They may have been glad to be rid of them for a few days or they might have caught a glimpse of the same vision their husbands had, we'll never know.

What is certain, however, is that the men had enough faith to go and their wives trusted them enough to let them have the good camels.

Dreaming of a Slushy Christmas

It never fails. We're standing in the middle of the floor, knee deep in a snake pit of Christmas lights. There are so many pieces missing from the artificial tree that it looks like it was clear cut. The kids have a Christmas list written out to Santa and ready to mail that Bill Gates couldn't afford to fill. The tires on the car are slicker than eel stuff and you've got to drive to Grandma's Christmas day or be cut out of the will. You get paid Christmas Eve about five p.m. and are thinking the only things that will be left in the stores will be some Tinker Toys and for some reason the wife is expecting a little more than that. You've still got to buy the turkey, the stocking stuffers and the presents for the in-laws and you withdrew the money from the Christmas savings back in August. It's colder than all get-out and you can't stand the cold. The furnace is acting like it might go out any minute.

So what are you dreaming of?

A white Christmas, of course.

There are several reasons we want a white Christmas:

1. Currier and Ives. These two jokers made snow popular during the holidays by romanticizing it. You will notice in all their prints that there is not one car in the ditch. Look at the people in those sleighs. They are not sober or they would not be smiling.

2. Snow cream. Legend has it that snow cream was accidently discovered in the Alps when a prehistoric hunter dropped some sugar and vanilla in the snow. Whatever the case, Southerners love it, even if they have

to scrape around the bird droppings to get the snow to make it.

3. We need a good snow to kill the bugs. Like the bugs hang around when it snows. The bugs are all in New Orleans. The only bugs the snow has ever killed were made by Volkswagen.

4. We all have sleds. It's true. We have sleds, brand new sleds that we bought when it last snowed. We all took them out to the hill at the school, slid straight down to the football field, where we all were buried head first in three feet of red mud. Then we took the sleds home. So we have them. In case it ever snows again.

There is an ugly rumor that we can't drive in the snow. It's not like we Southerners couldn't learn to drive in the snow. It's just that we never get a chance. And when we do, watch out.

First, we go about creating the ever popular three-rut road. This is accomplished when the first car, heading north, drives with its left tires where the center line would be if you could see it. The cars heading south also drive with their left tires in the center of the road. This forms a three-rut road and makes for some interesting driving as autos meet each other.

Next, we never drive over one and a half miles an hour. This is so that we can never build up enough speed to get any traction and spend most of our time spinning our wheels and sliding back and forth.

If we do get up any speed, we like to apply our brakes briskly and suddenly.

The North has snow plows and all sorts of snow removal equipment at its disposal. Most municipalities in the South have an old shovel and some ice cream salt. We do have, however, three or four guys per community who ride around drinking beer in four wheel drive vehicles. They will pull you out of the ditch or run you in it according to their mood.

People will tell you that if the weatherman is calling for snow, the best thing for you to do is to get out the sun tan lotion. This is because there has only been one correct prediction of snow in recent history. Usually we are pretty snug in our knowledge that "if they say it isn't coming, watch out."

But privately, just as soon as we hear the word snow mentioned, we are all obligated to report to the nearest grocery store immediately. This is because many Southerners starved to death in a blizzard during the Civil War when they came home with Moon Pies instead of stocking up on bread and milk. If you get a good dusting of snow today, you have to have a couple of loaves of bread and a good milk cow or you're doomed.

There is a law in the South that if snow is spotted (and we have authorized snow spotters on duty twelve months of the year) schools are to be shut down immediately. Mind you, this is if snow is spotted anywhere in a two hundred mile radius of the school.

We call off schools because we don't want our kids riding home in the snow on those dangerous school buses. Then we put them on a garbage can lid, tie it to the back bumper of the pick up and pull them around on the interstate. It's great fun.

So, we're all dreaming of a white Christmas. And just as soon as it snows, we'll heat up some cider and throw a couple of logs on the fire. Except the power will be off, so forget the hot cider. We didn't get a chance to buy any cider anyway because we couldn't get the car out of the driveway to go to the grocery store. So we'll cuddle up on the couch in the dark and watch as the bird's nest in the chimney catches fire. We'd call the fire department, but the phone lines are down.

This will probably be a good time to throw the Currier and Ives prints on the fire.

Organizing for the New Year

The New Year is just that: A new year, a new beginning, a fresh start, with hope for the future and expectations that your life will change for the better.

I say this because Sandra Claus gave me a really neat genuine leather-like case for Christmas. Now you're probably thinking that there's not a whole lot of hope or great expectations in a leather-like case and you may be a lot closer to the truth than you could ever know.

But don't tell Sandra.

You see, the case holds a devious "Week at a Glance" handy planner. The doggoned thing has every fifteen minutes of every day of the year (and part of next year) laid out so you can plan the minutest detail of your life.

And, no, I haven't lost it yet.

"It looks like Sandra would know you better than that," a co-worker said after I'd shared the fact that I had received something for Christmas to help me become organized.

"She does," I told her, "she just doesn't give up on me. She's an eternal optimist. After all, I do hang all my clothes in the same direction in the closet now. My desk, of course, still looks like Hurricane Fran ransacked it. But there's always hope."

There was a general convulsion of co-workers for awhile until they all gained control of themselves. They all know that Scarlett O'Hara ("Tomorrow is another day") is my patron saint and that procrastination is my religion.

So this doesn't mean just because I've got an "Every Fifteen Minutes of the Rest of Your Life Planner" that I'm making a New Year's resolution to be more organized. The statute of limitations has run out on resolutions, anyway, and I'm on the FBI's Ten Most All-Time Wanted List of Resolution Breakers, so that's out of the question.

I do recognize the need to be organized and I know it would come in handy in the mornings when I go to look for my shoes. So I'm going to give it another try.

Having been an old hand at resolutions I have learned something from the New Year's resolution experts. That's the great thing about America, we have experts on everything.

The experts tell you that if you're going to change your lifestyle, there are a series of steps you should take to be successful. If I'd had these earlier in life I could have probably already won the Publisher's Clearing House Sweepstakes because for years this was not only my financial plan but also my standard New Year's resolution.

Experts tell us that we should set realistic goals, the key word here being realistic. So I decided that maybe I should downsize my goal from the catch-all "getting organized" to the more realistic "finding my desk".

Another step toward realizing your goals is to develop a plan. Experts tell you to come up with some kind of scheme to counteract your bad habits.

So, I asked myself, is this really such a bad habit? I mean, one bad enough to warrant such extreme measures as sitting down and formulating a plan? The answer, of course, is relative. If you don't care if you never see your desk again, then it's not so bad. On the other hand, if there's a good chance your wife will kill you and bury your carcass under the stuff on your desk, you might want to give it a shot.

One key step in changing your complete lifestyle is to make sure the time is right. That's why so many resolutions fail. January 1 is not always the correct time for a major change in your life.

I looked at the offending desk. Maybe, I thought, February 1 would be a better time to begin getting organized. I located, with some difficulty, the trusty "Week at a Glance Planner, Organizer and Torturer" in its leather-like simulated plastic case. Under February 1 at 7:15 p.m. I wrote (in red) "get organized".

I felt better already.

For good measure, I added a footnote: "Look under bed for shoes."

Out Late With the Platters

Fifty-something columnist to twenty-something stepdaughter:

"We're going to see The Platters this Valentine's Day."

Twenty something step-daughter:

"Why?"

A good question, worthy of an answer, if I had one. To relive our past? To enjoy some great romantic '50s music? To have something to do besides eat on a Saturday night?

Someone in the midst of their '20s certainly would not understand any of this, much less the magic "The Great Pretender" or "Only You" brought to a generation.

As a member of the Platters once remarked: "I'll bet some of you have children because of this music."

But then twenty-something step-daughter said something quite unsettling.

"Besides," she added, "I thought the Platters were dead."

"Dead?" I stuttered. "They can't be dead. I just saw them in Chapel Hill in the '60s and they were alive and vibrant."

Well, maybe alive and not so vibrant, but I had just seen them that very short while ago. Could they have died young, in the prime of life? Perhaps in a plane crash. Or did they have planes back then?

And if so, I wondered who was performing in their place Valentine's night, under their name. We would soon find out.

Of course, we had to eat first, that being our generation's social life. The generation whose social life was once circling teenage hot spots with names like Brownie-Lu's, Liberty Drive-In, Dog and Suds and Melvin's has now come down to eating out. We've come a long way.

I told a couple of our friends that I bet they would be shagging before the night was over. David and Larry said they wanted to, but their wives wouldn't let them. I knew that David and Larry had legs like mine. When the music began, they locked up tighter than a mule's.

"We took one shagging lesson," said Jeanie, rolling her eyes, "and the instructor quit."

I surmised that after seeing them in action, he probably changed careers. Probably went into the ministry.

The Platters were appearing at the community center in a small nearby town. As we took our seats, I told Walter there certainly were a lot of old people there. Walter nodded. He looked good, just having had his toupee dry-cleaned for the occasion.

"If you think this crowd looks old," said Sandra, "don't look in the mirror when you go to the rest room."

But they did look old. There were a lot of gray heads, those who did have hair. There certainly hadn't been a lot of Rogaine usage among them. And there was no shortage of pot bellies in the audience. The men didn't look much better, either.

Someone in a our crowd wanted a Rolaid, but not even Susan, with her Pharmaceutical Satchel, had one.

After sitting in the folding chairs for half an hour waiting for the Platters to show up, part of the audience began clapping rhythmically.

"They're trying to get them to start the show," said David. "It's 8:00, they're getting sleepy."

Someone made an announcement that a blue Continental was in the parking lot with its lights on. Five or six people got up and went out. If this had been 1967, I thought, the announcement would have been for a yellow Volkswagen. And no one would have gotten up.

The lady beside me told me that she had just started a class on Rock 'n' Roll and had just learned that three of the Platters were dead. Counting in my head quickly, I figured that left only one and decided this might be a dull show.

I mentioned to her that it must have been a tragedy, people in their prime of life dying like that. She just stared at me.

We saw that a couple of young people had sneaked into the auditorium. More history students, Sandra said, doing research.

Finally the Platters came out. They sang some old Platters songs, plus others, including some by the Drifters, the Temptations and even Judy Garland's "Somewhere Over the Rainbow." When they left for a 15-minute intermission, David figured that they were going backstage for some Geritol.

The sound system was slightly substandard, making the songs touted as the music with words you could understand, hard to understand. Walter said maybe we needed new batteries for our hearing aids.

After intermission, the Platters introduced themselves. Only the lead singer, Monroe, was anywhere near being an original Platter. He was only the third lead singer the group had ever had, having started with the Inkspots. Monroe went way back, but didn't look it.

Finally the Platters ended their show, thanking everyone for coming, still on the stage playing as if they would play one more tune for a standing ovation.

But the crowd stood up as one, and began to filter out the exits of the community center. This audience was going home. It was past its bedtime.

Keeping Up With the House

I can remember when we used to take Easter Monday and work around the house. We might paint one year, caulk around the storm windows the next year.

That was before we bought the house locally known as "The Money Pit". Now we work all year long.

We should have been suspicious when we first purchased the house and saw that it had a private contractor's entrance.

But at least when you buy a house, you have something to show for it.

They call it "buyer's remorse", that sense of dread and despair and hopelessness that befalls you once you've made a rather large purchase and realize that, hey, you're stuck with it, payments and all.

This buyer's remorse thing hit me after I'd purchased the Computer from Hades and suddenly realized that I'd never paid so much for something so small and full of so many torments.

It hit me when I bought my first new car and saw, as I scribbled my signature on the "You Have Sold Your Soul and First Born Son Sales Agreement" that my monthly payment was more than my weekly salary.

But, according to those in the know, buyer's remorse really snags you right after you've signed that home mortgage and the seller, real estate agent and your lawyer stand up and give each other high fives.

You look down at this one-inch pile of forms you're signing and notice that there are 40 items under "Buyer

Pays", including "real estate agent's manicure and hairdo" and they all total your annual salary.

Under "Seller Pays" there might be one item, listed under "kickback to buyer's lawyer".

All this doesn't include, of course, the selling price of the home, which you have ingeniously talked the seller into dropping by fifty cents.

In the range of stressful life events, experts say that buying a home ranks eighth, right up there with the death of a spouse, teenager learning to drive, teenager living in house with you, marriage, divorce, buying a computer and being out of ice cream after the store has closed.

So now we "own our home", which obviously is a phrase the bank made up to make you think "you have something to show for it".

We wanted an older home because they have more personality than the new ones. You may have run across this personality thing before, like when you were dating and your friends (soon to be former friends) fixed you up with a blind date.

"He (or she) has a great personality," they'd say.

Sure, you'd think to yourself, and I bet they bark like a dog.

Personality, in a home, means the pipes knock late at night as if they have a life of their own. We have lived in ours now for over five years and I have finally been relieved of the duty of going under the house to see if someone with a hammer is actually living in our crawl space.

Personality means that you learn how to flush the commodes so they'll cut off in a reasonable amount of time.

Or that the noises you hear, like doors opening and closing in the otherwise quiet of the night are not intruders, just personality. Or ghosts of mortgage collectors.

Stuff breaks down, like the central air, which lasted for about five seconds after the ink dried on the sales agreement. Or the electric range.

"Our electric range is broken," Sandra lamented one day, with some anxiety.

Now I could expect something we used everyday like our charge cards or the defrost setting on the microwave to fall apart, but not the range. Our range is a pampered appliance and has barely been broken in good.

But Sandra was certain it was broken. She'd gotten cold in the kitchen one morning and decided to warm herself by turning on the oven and standing by the open door.

Sure enough, the oven didn't come on. We punched the button on the phone that automatically dials "appliance repairman". When you own a house like ours, you have these numbers pre-set.

A first responder repairman came right over. He looked at our stove and shook his head.

"Your range is a 1964 model," he told us sadly. "I'm afraid there's nothing I can do for it."

"But we never use it except for special occasions," I told him.

"What you don't use, you lose," he replied, giving me a good looking over. I wondered if he knew I was a '46 model.

But the biggest personality trait our house has is the paint, or the lack thereof.

When we first purchased the house, it was decided that I would paint the house "when needed" in order to save money. I don't remember exactly who decided this, but I'm fairly certain it wasn't me.

You may be interested to know that the Golden Gate Bridge is painted constantly, 365 days a year, because when the crew gets to the end, the other side needs painting again.

Our house is the Golden Gate Bridge of Homes. It peels faster than a sunburned back. A snake keeps its skin longer. It draws vinyl siding salesmen like flies to honey.

Last year, I painted through three seasons and would have painted through the winter had not Christmas interfered. Sandra would pass by occasionally to mention that she'd just watched some home improvement show on PBS and the guy had painted an entire house in half an hour.

The best part of home ownership, I guess, is that you get to help so many people in the community as an endless stream of exterminators, plumbers and electricians each leave a pile of bills by your door.

You definitely have, as they say, something to show for it.

Mother's Day

Mother's Day always gives me a chance to do something I rarely get to do any other time of the year. That is to wander aimlessly through the mall from one women's store to another praying for divine guidance.

You have to pray for guidance at the mall. Believe me, this is the only way you're going to get any help. Nowhere else can so many people be ignored so long by so few.

Shopping at the mall gives you several advantages. You get free parking, a choice of a variety of stores, all of which look strangely alike, and a food court swarming with teenagers.

Anyway, I wanted to buy Mom clothes for Mother's Day, so I went to the mall. One lesson I learned long ago is to stay out of the hardware store on Mother's Day. Women like frivolities on special occasions, not toaster ovens. This could well explain why Mom threw that toaster oven at you last Mother's Day.

And in case you missed Mother's Day, this may explain why Mom changed the locks on her doors. You can miss a Fourth of July now and then, but you don't want to miss a Mother's Day.

My mall trip was enlightening. If you need peace and quiet and don't want to be bothered by anyone, you should go walking through the stores in the mall. It's pretty good therapy.

Most of the stores keep a small staff to watch the cash register, put up stock and to make any customer who asks a question to feel like pond scum. These clerks are highly trained in taking your money and folding clothes.

Salespeople in malls are also skilled in not making eye contact with you. Try it sometime. You'll think these stores are operated by the Industries for the Blind.

I roamed around the mall awhile marveling at the bright spring fashions. I'd never seen such bold neon colors, pinks, purples, opalescent greens, iridescent blues and phosphorescent yellows.

I finally talked a salesman into helping me after I trapped him coming out of the rest room.

"I'm looking for a Mother's Day present," I told him.

"Well, what are you doing in the men's department?" he asked helpfully. I sulked past the radiant clothes to what looked like the women's department. At least this department was guarded by women.

I tricked one saleswoman into approaching me by pretending to shoplift something. This gets their attention every time. I told her I was looking for a Mother's Day present.

"Everything we have is on display," she said obligingly. "If I can be of assistance, just let me know."

There's one thing about the mall. You don't have to worry about pushy salespeople.

I looked around for awhile between the Sports section, the Adolescent department, Misses, Bridal, Maternity, Matron division, Women's bureau, Mrs. section and Ms. group. There was also a place for the well built woman and the well fed woman.

The more I looked the more confused I got. A nice pair of shorts, although a little too short for Mom, turned out to be a mini-skirt.

Finally a saleswoman came over to help me.

"We're closing," she said helpfully. "You'll have to leave." She had on one of those log chains to keep her glasses from sliding off her nose into eternity. I told her my problem.

"What size does she wear?" she asked. "We have 30, 32, 34's...then some clothes come in sizes like 10, 12, 14. Others come in medium and large, while some use Roman Numerals or codes only the CIA would understand."

I told her I thought Mom would like one of those blouses that have the NFL-type shoulder pads in them. That way she could go around all day with her shoulders humped up like she'd seen a rat or something.

"Well, if you find anything, let me know," she said helpfully.

I went off to look for the cookware section.

Greeting Cards

The great thing about greeting cards is that they will say what you never had the nerve (nor the faintest idea, in some cases) to say. And they will say it for under four dollars plus postage in most cases.

Letter writing may be dead, but card sending is alive and well in America. For most of us, greeting cards offer a way to say what we mean without having to sit down and come up with something on our own. The card people know very well that we are having trouble expressing our feelings and that even if we could, we just don't have the time to mess with it.

Speaking of time, I could write a novel faster than I can pick out a card. I might start out with the Valentine's cards, but eventually I'll drift down to the birthday cards. It's like a card undertow had a hold of you. And I'll get to laughing at the birthday cards and eventually buy two or three, plus some anniversary cards, just to have in emergencies.

I'm amazed at the wide range of greeting cards now. There are cards for every occasion you've ever thought of and some that aren't occasions yet, but soon will be.

There are cards that say "Just a Card to Say Hi", "Just a Card to Say Goodbye" and "Just a Card to Say We Missed You at the Poker Game".

Greeting cards are so specialized now. You can buy a Valentine's card for your mechanic ("You Make My Motor Purr"), for your bank teller, your bookie and even your cat. You can get one for your letter carrier ("I'd Play Post Office With You"), your golf pro or your grocer.

One of my favorites is the one in which the man is standing on the kitchen table in his raincoat flashing his wife while she's washing the dishes.

"For Godsakes, just bring me the dirty dishes," she says. Must be a married couple.

There are a lot of cards that say "Sorry I Haven't Written Lately". What they mean is "Sorry I Haven't Sent You a Card Lately" because nobody writes anymore. The slowest sellers in the card line are bound to be the blank cards in which you have to make up your own greeting.

There are Bon Voyage cards for friends who are moving. There are cards that say "Glad You're Back". There are even "Glad You're Gone and Good Riddance" cards.

Birthday and Get Well cards make up the great majority of cards. You can find a birthday card for any age and condition. The best ones are the cards for the over forty set, the ones of us who are on the down hill slide. All the rest are boring, with little rainbows or stars or unicorns and snappy little lies like "When You Were Born, They Broke The Mold". What they really mean is "When You Were Born, Daddy Had a Vasectomy".

Get Well cards are good. There's a different section for every illness, in alphabetical order, with categories for hospital stays and surgeries. These have catchy little phrases, like "Hope Your Hemorrhoids Are Healing" and "Congratulations on the Successful Sex Change Operation".

There are Divorce cards: "Glad to Hear You're Divorced" and "Glad to Hear We're Divorced".

You can find cards to boyfriends, with sub-categories "from female" and "from male". If your sister's husband's aunt's cousin is sick, believe me, there's a card for you.

There are cheery cards ("Cheer Up, That Hangover Won't Last Forever" or "Cheer Up, A Lot of Wives Shoot Their Husbands").

As if they weren't selling enough cards, many greeting card companies have begun to create holidays so that we can send more cards. I have a feeling Grandparents Day started like this. Next we'll have First Cousin Day, Dog Days and Garbage Man Day. I have also seen some Veteran's Day and Groundhog's Day cards popping up lately. Can Labor Day cards be far behind?

Of all the cards, Christmas cards are my favorites. Every year I go shopping early, intentionally looking for funny Christmas cards. Everything else can wait until the last minute (including mailing them) but I've got to have those funny cards.

One year I came across the best one I've ever found. It was a hand-made, photocopied job but, as they say in the greeting card circles, when they made this one they broke the mold. It simply said:

"Money is tight,

"Times are hard,

"Here's your _____ed old Christmas card."

Ah, those greeting cards are poetry to my ears.

The Annual Graduation Harangue

It's time for the long-awaited annual keepsake ready-to-cut-out-and-put-in-your-scrapbook graduation guide and advice commentary. It seems like these things roll around every year.

Last year's graduation essay was such a hit that I've been personally asked to do another one. I heard that last year's advice so touched the graduating seniors that they cut it out and lined their car trunks with it before they took off to the beach. So if you don't want them cutting up this book, you'd better buy them a book of their own. Heck, buy them two books so they'll have a spare.

What would graduation be without advice? Advice is to todays graduate as water is to a duck's back. I'd be willing to wager big bucks that none of you have a clue as to either: 1. Who your graduation speaker was. 2. What he said. I'd bet if Moses was your graduation speaker, you wouldn't remember what he said much less what was on those tablets. You remember that your friend Herbert went naked under his gown, but anything relevant has eluded you.

We all like to give our kids advice so that later we can say "I told you so". Advice is about the freest and easiest thing you can get this side of mosquitoes in the summertime. People who won't give you the time of day will gladly pass on a piece of advice and you don't even have to ask them for it. The only thing you can get any cheaper than advice is the weather report and both are liable to be wrong.

A graduation ceremony is the best place on earth to hear advice. Everyone is there. Most parents come because they are proud. Then there is a sizable contingent who come because they are in shock. Teachers come because they are proud, too, but some come just to make sure the graduating seniors do leave.

Then there are those who, like the man whose enemy had died, said that although he wouldn't attend the funeral, he certainly approved of it. Teachers approve of graduation because it keeps an even flow of students and insures that they don't get the same troublesome bunch next year.

Speakers have a captive audience at graduation: The parents. The only reason the seniors are there is that the school won't mail their diplomas to the beach. A speaker could stand in front of a bunch of graduates and mumble the words to Beethoven's Fifth Symphony (there are words, aren't there?) and the graduates would applaud wildly, grab their diplomas and head for Myrtle Beach.

Advice, or even the threat of it, has that effect on people.

I don't know why any of us think kids will pay attention to the same tired advice we ignored when we were their age. Are our memories really that dim? To most of us, advice is the road map we finally pick up after we've reached our destination.

Mark Twain said that "All you need in this life is ignorance and confidence; then success is sure." The only trouble with this is that, after a certain age, most of us are no longer ignorant. We become smart enough to know that we can't do it. With this knowledge comes loss of confidence. Our youth, many of whom are among our graduating seniors, are just dumb enough to think they can succeed in this world. Luckily for them they have us adults to tell them they can't.

We are constantly telling our youth that they are too young. And while we're keeping them from taking a chance on succeeding, they're growing old enough to learn that they can't succeed on their own.

If I had the chance to speak to a graduating class, this would be my advice:

Be careful in what you ask for. You may receive it. Success and failure can both be hard to take. Make a difference in the world. Don't just go with the status quo.

Don't be too serious about life that you can't laugh at yourself. If you go to college, don't let your studies interfere with your education. And if you don't go to college, don't quit learning. You never quit learning.

In the next ten years, you will probably do something utterly stupid. Learn from it and make something good come from it.

In the ten next years or so you will lose someone you care something about. Tell them you care something about them now. And stop to smell the flowers now and then. Even if you are allergic to them.

Don't be afraid to march to the beat of a different drummer. If you've ever noticed, the people who make a difference are different.

Do it now. Or, as Jonathan Swift said: "May you live all the days of your life."

And don't overdose on all the advice you're going to get.

A Short Graduation Test

1. What if you open your diploma after you're seated and find a blank piece of paper?
   A. You probably have a collector's item.
   B. This means you can write anything on it you want to.
   C. That dumb principal goofed again.
   D. The bribe you gave the Biology teacher didn't work.
2. Graduation means:
   A. Going to the beach.
   B. I can carry my gun anywhere I please now.
   C. I won't have to miss The Price is Right
   D. I won't have to eat bad food like they served in the cafeteria because I'm getting married.
3. Which is correct?
   A. I won't have to study no more English.
   B. I won't have to study English no more.
   C. I won't have to study English no more, dude.
4. What should you do when your child crosses the stage?
   A. Yell, "Way to go Herbert! We knowed you could do it."
   B. Hide under the bleachers and shout "Whoo-eee".
   C. Throw firecrackers at the band.
   D. Continue to talk loudly just as you did when the other graduates got their diplomas.
5. The best parties after graduation are at:
   A. Myrtle Beach
   B. Ft. Lauderdale
   C. Daytona Beach

    D. East Carolina University

    (Hint: One of these is a four year party)

6. The best thing about graduation for parents is:
    A. The kids will be home all day long now.
    B. You get to shell out $100,000 for college.
    C. They get to go to the beach and you don't.
    D. They can hang their tassel on your rear view mirror.

7. In case of thunder storms during the ceremonies:
    A. All faculty will be asked to sit in the metal bleachers.
    B. Your gun may get wet.
    C. Be sure to wear underwear because you can see right through a wet gown.
    D. Everyone will march in orderly fashion to the conveniently un-air conditioned gym.

A Politically Correct Fourth of July

Two hundred and twenty some years ago our Founding Fathers signed the Declaration of Independence. It was a time when common men acted with uncommon courage. You have to wonder, though, what would have happened in 1776 had things gone a tad differently.

The colonists, of course, wanted their freedom from England for many reasons: harsh laws, taxation without representation, the fact that government officials could walk right into their homes or ships without a warrant to look for smuggled goods, and the burden of having to keep up the British army in the colonies in a time of peace.

This anger culminated at the Boston Tea Party in 1773, when a group of men dressed as Indians dumped a load of tea into the Boston harbor.

Before dawn, however, the Native American Antidefamation and Saturday Night Bingo League had filed a lawsuit in Federal court against these citizens, claiming their actions belittled, libeled and otherwise insulted the various Indian tribes of America. One of the colonists was found to be wearing a Washington Redskins sweatshirt under his Indian disguise, which complicated matters. A Congressional panel convened to determine how to better serve the Indian population and it was decided to kill most of them off and then apologize to the rest.

The EPA filed an unrelated suit several days later claiming that the band of men had polluted the harbor, causing a rather large fish kill and rendering the water unfit to drink except by people highly addicted to caffeine.

The Food and Drug Administration charged that tea was a drug and thus should be regulated by the Federal government. The FDA proposed a ban on all sales of tea to minors and suggested curtailing all advertising at the popular Camp Town Races, which was on the Tea Cup Circuit.

The defendants in the Boston Tea Party Fiasco, as it was later known, hired the firm of Adams, Adams and Monroe and after a widely publicized trial, were found not guilty in criminal court. They were later tried in civil court, found liable for damages, filed bankruptcy and wrote best selling books.

President Washington, himself in trouble over Cherrytreegate, finally pardoned the entire bunch.

Conspiracy buffs charged that the Lipton Tea Company had paid the colonists to dump tea into the harbor in a price-fixing scheme. The government, however, claimed that the men were actually test dummies dropped from high altitude.

In 1775 British troops came upon a company of American militia at Lexington. Paul Revere had tried to warn the colonists that the British were coming, but animal rights activists had stopped him and had him arrested for mistreatment of his horse.

The American militia were busy burning their draft cards when the British surprised them and many scattered for Canada. Others became school teachers until the fighting was over. Those who did stand and fight were later ridiculed for having fought in an unpopular war. Later a monument was built to appease the veterans.

Finally, representatives of the thirteen colonies, at least those not under Federal indictments for campaign fund violations, met in Philadelphia. Immediately several were caught accepting bribes in an FBI sting.

Thomas Jefferson was nominated to write a sort of declaration of freedom from the British crown, but was distracted by a bomb threat when a Ryder Rental truck was found parked outside his bedroom window.

Ben Franklin was accosted as he left his apartment by an angry crowd demanding several concessions and screaming "we pay your salary, we pay your salary." Franklin scattered the crowd when he tried to collect his wages from them, stating he hadn't been paid in years. Later he was sentenced for using deceptive practices in marketing lightning rods.

The Baptists boycotted the proceedings, accusing one of the New Jersey representatives of "dressing in women's clothes and other foul practices."

Jefferson, having finished the declaration under doctor's care (medicinal marijuana) was berated by the NRA for being weak on guns and his "all men are created equal" phrase was thrown out because it failed to mention anyone but white males. The American Agnostic Society protested the use of "Creator" and "God" in the declaration.

Jefferson became depressed and appeared several times on the Jerry Springer show before finally committing suicide.

John Hancock was caught in a motel room with Dolly Madison. The rest is history.

Happy Fourth of July.

Cooking Out and Other Afflictions

The long awaited summer time is here and with it comes the afflictions of the season: mosquitoes, Japanese beetles, sunburn, humidity, yard mowing and cooking out.

The tradition of cooking out began sometime several years ago when early man discovered fire. If electricity had been discovered first, we probably wouldn't be burdened with this cooking out craze, or at least we would have barbecue grills with extension cords.

But, no, we had to go discover fire first.

Early man quickly realized that cooked meat, even burned meat, was preferable to raw meat. Scientists speculate that this happened when some Neanderthal, smoking in bed, burned the cave down along with the contents of the refrigerator.

Cooking out caught on after this and continued for many years. Then cooking in was discovered to be even better because green flies didn't fall in your food as often. Cooking in, however, was found to be more dangerous and resulted in the invention of the fire department.

Cooking in became so popular that cooking out was relegated to cattle drives, hunting trips, prison escapees, hobos and Boy Scout Camporees. Since it was mostly men who were involved in these pursuits, two popular misconceptions arose: 1. That men were good at cooking out. 2. That men actually enjoyed cooking out.

No one thought much about cooking out at home, however, until the invention of the back yard, a concoction of your National Lawn Mowing Association to help sell more lawn mowers. It was difficult to work up an appetite among the chickens, hound dogs, bee hives and outdoor facilities that were commonly found behind the house. The backyard changed all that. To the uninitiated, it may seem that we have gone backwards a bit in this cooking out craze. The uneducated person may think that once cooking moved inside, it should have stayed inside where conditions were cleaner, more sanitary and easier controlled. This, of course, shows a nonprogressive attitude. Today, we have available on the market $3500 grills. The grill has in fact become like the car. Everybody wants the biggest and the best. Many retailers offer stainless steel features and non-traditional colors such as hunter green, cherry red and burgundy. One model, at $2500, includes side shelves, a slide-out bottom tray, six burners and, for $349 more, a side-mounted rangetop burner.

At our house we feature the Rose-O-Matic Grill, purchased in 1987 at a price of $9.99. It came in the non-traditional color of Morbid Black.

Most of our friends have progressed to the gas grill, but none of them have gone to the four-figure models. Basically the one benefit of the gas grill I can see is that you can immediately burn the meat and burn it more evenly. One has to wait awhile for the charcoal to get hot enough to burn anything. Of course, with the gas grill, you don't get to exclaim "those coals are just right for steaks" two hours after your meal is finished.

There are several mysteries to life: Why anyone would think that a man who cannot boil water on an electric range would be a master chef once he gets outside on the grill; why anyone who would not let the tiniest gnat inside her kitchen would proclaim, once outside, that "those things on the hamburger are probably onion sprinkles"; and why anyone would ask the griller "when will they be ready?" and actually expect him to know within an hour or so.

The only fact I know for certain is that at least two hamburgers will fall into the coals during grilling. I have grown so confident of this that now I just throw two in there for starters so I won't have to be bothered with them later.

And I know those fancy grills may make cooking out easier and more fun, but for sheer excitement and adventure, I'll stick to my ten dollar job.

Sandra says the Neanderthals would have been proud of me.

A Trip to the Big Apple

I wanted to spend the Fourth of July in the United States, but Sandra wanted to go to New York City.
NEW YORK CITY?
I did everything I could to talk her out of it. Told her we would have to forgo the annual Eat Till You Die Homemade Ice Cream Fest. Noted that we wouldn't get to see the firing of the bottle rockets down the street or listen to the birdshot fall on the roof when the neighbors fired their shotguns. Even mentioned that we would miss the celebration at nearby Snow Camp where you could get country ham biscuits.
"You can't get country ham biscuits in New York," I told her.
But she wouldn't budge. Besides, she said, it wasn't like we were going alone. We would have cultured friends along with us, plus an entire tour bus of people from the area.
This business about the cultured friends excited me until I found out they had been replaced by Bud, Peggy, Walter and Susan.
Just as soon as people began finding out we were going to New York, we began to get advice. Don't look up. Don't look anyone in the eye. Don't act like you're lost. Don't leave your group.
I began to feel like the baby antelope on the Wild World of Animals that leaves the herd and becomes lion lunch.

The tour we finally decided on was scheduled to spend three nights at a world class hotel, right across from Madison Square Garden. Although Bud's AAA Guide Book of New York City didn't list the hotel, we didn't see this as a problem. Probably too nice to be listed, I figured. Or newly built. Or a typographical error.

Or, so it turned out, Omen Number One.

We boarded our air conditioned, restroom equipped motorcoach at 6:30 a.m. on July 4. The first thing we were told was not to use the restroom because what we left in it would stay with us for the entire three days. Twenty people immediately got up to use the restroom. The driver casually mentioned that he had never been to New York City, but he was willing to give it a try. Omen Number Two.

Our first of many rest and meal stops was at a restaurant where we ate breakfast and were finally served our drinks as we were re-boarding the bus. The omens were piling up faster than antelope carcasses, but it was too late to abandon ship.

The tour director explained that they did not pass out name tags on the New York trip because they "did not want anyone to know we were tourists." I thought this was pretty smart considering we were all dressed in Bermudas, white socks, brand new tennis shoes and had cameras around our necks. Those who didn't have new shoes still had red mud on theirs. All this and riding in a bus that read "I like calling North Carolina home." Boy, they'd never spot us.

A couple of hours into the journey was spent playing Bingo for coveted refrigerator magnets and pens. The rest was spent trying to sleep balled up like Wilt Chamberlain in a seat built for Tiny Tim.

After an all day ride we finally saw the New York City skyline. This is where our bus driver stopped dead on the side of the New Jersey Turnpike and tried to call our hotel for directions on his cellular phone. There was no answer at our hotel, but by this time I had quit counting omens. I had, however, memorized all the locations of the exits on the bus and swallowed our itinerary in case we were captured.

Unperturbed, our driver drove on awhile, then picked an exit at random and drove down it with the exuberance of a drowning man. It soon became apparent that we were in the heart of Harlem and after cruising around awhile viewing the scenic graffiti, concentina wire and spray painted signs on doorways that read "Pit Bull--Stand Back", he decided we were lost.

I figured we were mighty lucky we didn't have our name tags on.

Someone toward the back of the bus (I think it was Peggy) was mumbling "we're gonna die, we're gonna die." This is when our intrepid driver did what all good men do after riding around lost for half an hour. He stopped to ask directions. And lo and behold, a real New Yorker (the manager of a McDonalds) actually got in his car and led the bus out of Harlem. Well, not exactly out of Harlem, but out of the part of Harlem where you can die in daylight to the part where you can only die at night.

We arrived at our hotel around 7:30, got our keys and headed for our rooms. The hotel, by the way, was built in 1919. It's motto, widely known around the city, is "The Same Carpet For Almost A Hundred Years."

The word "room" is often misleading, making one think that there is actually room, or space, there to, say, sit down. Not necessarily so. Our "room" was eight feet wide. The TV was jammed between the bed and the wall along with a dresser and two chairs. One chair got in the way when you wanted to do something extraordinary, like walk. The bathroom had a shower, no stall, just a curtain that wrapped around your legs like it had static cling. When Sandra showered and I shaved, water hit me on the head from the shower. This way we both could wash our hair at the same time.

The size of the room would not have mattered so much had I not seen Walt and Susan's suite. Theirs had a king sized bed, wing chairs, couch, buffet, a large bathroom with a tub and some other small room, to be used for entertaining small parties of fifty or so, I guess. I wasn't jealous, but I did whisper a prayer that their bed would have bed bugs or at least lice.

We saw our first mouse that night while eating at a restaurant complex adjacent to the hotel. Bud, Peggy, Sandra and I had chosen to eat Nathan's hotdogs. Walt and Susan had decided to eat the exotic New York City hamburger, kept warm in water for three days and always a popular tourist attraction.

We saw many more mice at the hotel, not to mention some nice roaches. As a matter of fact, every room had critters but ours. Perhaps our room was too small for mice. If they were there, I guarantee they were hunchbacked.

We were all privileged to be in Walter's suite when their first mouse appeared. The ladies immediately jumped on the back of the couch because: 1. "A mouse can't get you there". 2. It was the only part of the couch that was dry.

Although I had not been overly jealous over the size of Walt's room, I did think that prayers are answered when I saw the rat appear.

Walter reluctantly called the desk to change rooms. The desk clerk said he would send "a real man" up to check out this mouse.

It became apparent why Walter was reluctant to change rooms when the move to a different room actually occurred. It was sort of like moving Macy's. Susan had brought every piece of clothing she owned and obviously had borrowed more from friends to bring along. I hadn't seen so many hangers in most dry cleaners. For a second I thought the trip had been scheduled for six months instead of three nights.

All in all, our friends moved so many times because of mice that we lost track of them. We decided that our room stunk to badly of old cigar smoke that no mouse would get near it. A pilot who was staying on our floor told us he was used to the mice. "Just keep your suitcase locked and your shoes on" he advised us.

Walter noted that the trip wasn't very expensive.

"And who said you don't get what you pay for?"

We took on a Broadway play while in the city. Susan was excited about this prospect because "The King and I" was playing and she wanted to see Yul Brenner. Some of us wanted to go see "Les Miserables", but none of us could pronounce it. We finally ended up seeing "Victor-Victoria" with Julie Andrews, mainly because Julie was still alive. Peggy noted that Henry Mancini had written the score for Victor-Victoria and wondered if he was directing the orchestra. I made a note to get Peg and Susan a "Guide to Dead People" as soon as we got home.

Even though they called it a theater, I could find no popcorn or Milk Duds anywhere. I did notice that everyone around us spoke a foreign language, so I finally asked the couple next to us where they were from.

"Brooklyn," they said.

Later we found a super New York deli with a buffet to die for. You paid for your plate by the pound and when they weighed Sandra's I heard the cashier tell the owner "we've got a new record".

As we were eating, someone noticed that Susan hadn't touched her food.

"I think I'm having a heart attack," Susan noted.

Walter, immediately sensing an emergency, began to eat faster.

"I've got some Tums," said Peggy.

"There's some Maalox in my purse," offered Sandra.

"Can I have your shrimp?" I asked.

Other highlights of the trip included:

Sandra buying a Rolex at Battery Park for $15.00. It lasted two weeks. I have advised her to write the nice Rolex representative she purchased it from for replacement.

Getting stuck on an elevator for five minutes.

Peggy mentioning that she hoped we didn't get "gridironed" in the traffic on the way home.

Our taxi rides with Mohammed-Abdul Earnhardt.

Our $42.00 breakfast.

One of our days in New York was scheduled to be an eight-hour tour of the city leaving at 8 a.m. By 9:30 our intrepid driver had still not showed up. We spent the time wisely, watching people on the street, some of whom insisted on eating out of the garbage cans. Watching the taxis it occurred to me that perhaps stock car racing hadn't really developed first in the South as we think. Later we learned that our driver had left his keys to the bus in a taxi and had to hire a locksmith to make him another key.

When we finally got going on our tour, our walk-on guide, Dave, a New York resident, admitted to me privately that "I love living in the city, but I have to escape now and then."

I have never heard the word "escape" used in talking of any other city in the world in peacetime and I think that word says it all.

That and the fact that as our bus left New York City, the entire group, including our tour director, cheered.

Talking the Talk

We thought for awhile about taking in the Summer Olympics in Atlanta, but then I realized that we might not speak the right language.

You see, they're selling out down in Atlanta. Selling out on their heritage, that is.

The same city that once was burned by Sherman is getting burned again, this time by some sharp entrepreneurs from Yankeeland.

Not that I have anything against Yankees, mind you. Yankees have contributed much to our culture and as soon as I come up with these accomplishments, I will publish them. Until then, you'll just have to take my word for it.

Anyway, it seems that Southern businessmen in Atlanta have been told their Southern accents are holding them back, especially in their dealing with Madison Avenue. Companies like Coke and AT&T are hiring speech therapists to help their employees sound less Southern. Others are taking "accent reduction" courses to lose their drawls and are being burned at the rate of $1,000 for this service.

"With a Southern accent, it's difficult to make a good first impression," one Atlanta accountant said.

"If you speak with a Southern accent, they think of you as less than bright," said an Atlanta ad man.

My question is why do you need to go to a class to talk to people who can't talk? These Peachtree Street Whizzes are paying $1,000 to talk to people who say "youse guys" and eat "ersters".

It looks like someone's been watching too many Beverly Hillbilly reruns.

It hasn't been so long ago that Northerners (or D. Yankees) discovered the sunny South and its many amenities. A few stayed here after the Civil War (Silver Wah, or The Late Unpleasantness) and immediately thought us to be less than bright because we ate most parts of a hog and sang songs like "Eating Goober Peas".

The real influx came after the development of the interstate highway system. Northern tourists could buzz down south without being encumbered by stop lights or any pretty scenery and many stayed here after finding out that our winters didn't last eleven months. They found the people to be friendly, the climate warmer, prices lower and lifestyles slower. For this reason they came down in droves and immediately began to attempt to change us.

These Northerners acted so strangely and talked so funny that a section, later named Florida, was set aside to house them all. Soon, however, many of these people began to leak out over the countryside and quickly spread over much of the Southland.

Every now and then one of our Southern friends would pick up this strange Northern accent. We might say they were "putting on airs" or that they had gotten a postcard from up north and had talked that way ever since.

But no one ever dreamed that this language would be taught on our own side of the Mason-Dixon Line. And it's probably being taught by people who once lived near "Toity-toid" Street in Brooklyn. Which reminds me of the Brooklyn schoolboy who, when told by his teacher that a sparrow wasn't a "boid" protested "But it choips like a boid."

Anyone who has ever been far from Dixie for any long period of time knows how good it is to get home and hear that good ole Southern drawl. It's music to your ears. When I came home from the Army after living in close quarters with foreigners from distant lands like Michigan and Chicago, I sounded like Sgt. Preston of the Yukon. I would have paid $1,000 to get my drawl back.

So it's hard to believe that people in Atlanta are paying to lose theirs. The next thing you know, someone will convince us that blondes, because they're dingy, need to dye their hair to make it in the business world. Or that brown-eyed folks, because they're devious, will have to wear blue contacts.

Maybe those Atlanta turncoats ought to realize that it's what you say, not how you say it, that matters. Judging a person by how he talks or dresses is a bad mistake, as most salespeople will readily tell you.

I don't care if they stand around in their boardrooms talking about how culture began in Bayonne and how some of us down here still don't have indoor plumbing. Freedom of speech means freedom to leave off your "g's" if you want. I'm certainly not trading in my "ya'll" for anyone.

As grandpa used to say: "I never seed th' beat."

If you want a translation, it'll cost you $1,000.

A Fish in the Hand

I don't remember who came up with the idea, but we all seemed to embrace it hook, line and sinker. We wanted to go fishing on Labor Day.

Fishing is a sport I've never dabbled in. I grew up in a family that hunted and we spent many autumn days in pursuit of the wily gray squirrel and the now extremely rare Chatham rabbit. Fishing involved too much standing still for me at that time in my life.

Now, the older I get, the more attractive standing still, or even sitting still, has become. In fact sitting still, one of the main requirements for fishing, has become one of my strong points.

Usually I prefer to sit down at a meal but I am also equally proficient at sitting in front of the TV. Sitting on a pond bank is something I could catch onto pretty quickly.

Just as soon as we came up with the fishing idea, problems presented themselves. For instance, none of us had any fishing equipment. I even made a trek to the dreaded storage building to verify this.

Sandra had been under the delusion that she had retained a rod and reel from her youth, but it was discovered that the Smithsonian had probably come for it years ago. It's featured, no doubt, in their Ancient Art of Fishing exhibit at this very moment.

So it seemed that we needed extensive gear for this outing. I figured this consisted (but was not limited to) rods, reels, line (known to avid fisherpersons as "monofilaments"), hooks, sinkers, bobbers, tackle boxes, waders and hats (to stick the hooks in). Maybe a boat. Life jackets. A trailer to tow the boat. A nice truck to hitch the trailer to.

I didn't add the filet knives and scalers simply because I didn't think we were in any danger of catching any keepers. Besides, there was no one in our party whose stove worked.

We needed bait, though. Our compost pile is full of nice juicy worms and other critters which I thought would suffice nicely. Sandra said she was thinking more in terms of something a little more artificial, maybe something in a plastic worm.

Erik, quite an avid fisherman and outdoorsman himself, told us he often fished with raw liver. This is a multi-purpose bait, he told us. Once he was fishing at Fontana, wasn't having much luck and was growing mighty hungry.

"We just cooked the liver," he said, "and ate it."

He didn't say whether or not said liver had been in the lake first.

Then someone mentioned fishing licenses.

Sandra seemed to think you didn't need one if you met certain requirements. I told her these requirements seemed to be that you were under age 16 and accompanied by an adult who had a license.

Someone else commented that you could probably get away with one fishing outing without a license.

I mentioned to them of the time when Willard and I went licenseless into the woods and came out with pink slips that cost us $75 apiece at a time when $75 was a good car payment. And we didn't even get to keep our quail.

"I'll spend the money to buy a Sportsman License (which includes the right to Buffalo hunt, by the way) before I'll go out without one," I told them.

I had turned into a law-abiding citizen in my old age. Getting caught will do that to you.

Finally we came to the realization that we needed somewhere to fish. We went over a number of local ponds, thinking surely one of these benevolent land owners would give us permission to fish for just one day.

Sandra brought up the issue of snakes and requested that the pond be "a clean one."

It was noted that some of the ponds were in cow pastures and presented the ever-present danger of "cow patties."

Someone else requested that we bring insect repellant because of mosquitoes and ticks. I added this to the list after the trolling motor.

Ed suggested that we could try fishing in the lagoon at the sewage treatment plant.

"I bet it's full of catfish," he volunteered.

"There's no fish in there," Sandra groaned, with the same look on her face as when the fishing worms were mentioned.

That's when it dawned on me that the fish weren't important. I had learned this lesson as a youngster hunting in Chatham County. The game you brought back was incidental to the sport. We weren't going to cook any fish, anyway.

It was the being out-of-doors that mattered, the comradery, the relaxation, the restoring of the soul, the planning.

Maybe, I thought, we ought to invest in a bass boat, too.

Traveling Without a Clue

Sandra and I had been thinking about taking a vacation for quite some time. As a matter of fact, the time had been "quite some" for so long that the last time we had a vacation the only place you could stop to use the bathroom was Stucky's.

That we needed and deserved a vacation was agreed upon. Sandra, however, wanted to take off and just head north and see what adventures lay ahead. I, on the other hand, like to plan every move, to chart each day like a navigator on a ship and to know, for instance, that I have a room and bath awaiting at the next stop.

Since we had tried my method on the last trip (to the best of my foggy memory, about a decade ago) it was decided that we try Sandra's idea this time. We would strike out in the general direction of Maine and see what the open road held for us. I did, however, manage to sneak out and buy an atlas of the United States just in case the open road became vague at some point.

Here is a short log I managed to keep (unbeknownst to Sandra) so that if our bodies were found in New Hampshire, people would know our story:

Day One: Finally leave home around lunch. I want to leave earlier, but forget that "we have no plans". Drive up Highway 81 through Shenandoah Valley in the rain. Luckily, I have thought ahead and coated the windshield with Rain-Go-Away, the patented formula that smears your windshield so that you can barely see. Either that or we need new windshield wipers.

We stop momentarily at Gettysburg, then drive over to Lancaster. Stop at four motels (driver getting very antsy) before we find a room at Rabbi Levi's Motel and Amish Recreation Center. Make mental note to start looking for room earlier in future.

Day Two: While sneaking a peek at a forbidden map, tell wife that there are many neat towns around, including Bird-in Hand, Gap, Paradise and Strasburg. Wife informs me that she wants to go to nearby K-Mart.

Ride around Amish countryside in rain. Amish, being smarter than tourists, are not out in rain. Head north through picturesque two-lane roads to New York state. Realize that the one thread that unites us all as a nation are the three words "Road Under Construction". Finally find room at Jacob Greenbalm's Motel and Mortuary. Make mental note to start looking for room earlier. Eat at Italian restaurant. People there guess we are from Arkansas.

Day Three: Ride up through Adirondacks in rain. View is probably lovely. Near Ft. Ticonderoga, we head into Vermont. If there is a prettier state than Vermont in the fall, I don't know of it. We secure a room at motel at a price that would make motel owners at Myrtle Beach on the Fourth of July envious. A half hour later, motel is turning away customers, telling them that "it's brutal on weekends this time of year." We learn that 'this time of year" is Columbus Day weekend, an unheard of holiday down South, but as big as Labor Day up North. We decide to stay two more nights. Everyone in Vermont looks like they came from an L.L. Bean reunion.

People guess that we are from Tennessee.

We notice a disturbing trend at restaurants. No sweetened tea. And waitresses don't refill your drink unless you have a court order.

Days Four and Five: Ride around Vermont in rain looking at covered bridges, magnificent leaves, white churches, inns, beautiful homes and farms. Try to disguise my voice. People think we are from northern Arkansas.

Visiting Vermont is like eating sugar, lots of sugar. After awhile, there is just so much you can take. We head for Maine in hopes of at least seeing some litter strewn highways to remind us of home.

Day Six: Pull into Ogunquit, an Indian word meaning "tourist trap." Columbus Day is over, Ogunquit has just ended its peak season and motel rooms are cheap and plentiful. We eat lobster. We almost dehydrate in restaurant waiting for glasses to be refilled with something the locals refer to as "tea".

Lady guesses we are from North Carolina.

Day Seven: Drive to Bar Harbor, Maine, which fortunately is still at the height of its tourist season so that rooms are triple what they should be. Make mistake of asking for "tea" and get hot tea. Farther north you go, worse tea gets. I imagine it tastes like mud in Canada.

We luckily get third floor overlooking bay for a little less than a new car payment. At 10:30, I hear terrible noise and look out to see ferry unloading cars and buses underneath our window. No wonder room is so cheap. Ferry is unloaded by 3 a.m. so that we are able to get our much needed rest.

Overhear lady telling her husband that Maine reminds her of Portugal.

Day Eight: Drive south through Maine. Stop at Burger King to sample local cuisine. Loudly tell wife it reminds me of Portugal. Wife kicks me under table. We inform people at Burger King that we are disappointed that we have been in Maine a whole day and have yet to see a moose. They direct us to a "near-by" state animal farm.

An hour and half later and three stops for directions, we find animal farm, snap quick picture of moose through chain link fence, and resume trip. Begin to plan how to convince friends that we saw wild moose in woods. Wife says we can "White Out" fence.

Wife realizes that camera has a "focus" on it.

People think we are from Alabama.

While bypassing Boston, we get caught in rush hour traffic heading into sun on three lane highway under construction with no lane markers. Realize where Broadway play title "Damned Yankees" came from. On third stop, find room at Marlboro, Mass. Finally realize that tea at Boston Tea Party was thrown overboard because it was so bad.

Day Nine: At 8:30 a.m. I convince wife that Lexington and Concord, where the Revolutionary War began, are only "this far" away from us on the map. Using navigational skills, I figure this is about 12 miles away. Wife questions where I came up with map. We negotiate commuter traffic on quaint two lane roads to these towns. Sixty miles out of our way and two hours later, we finally head home. Wife confiscates map.

Day Ten: Grant, Pa. We have learned to stop at Holiday Inns, which are always full, where they will tell us of the nearest motel vacancies. Finally realize that Northerners are almost always ill because of the tea they drink.

Day Eleven: Home. Run into the worst drivers on trip, those on I-40 in North Carolina. Know we are home when we see roadside litter. Can't wait to drink sweetened tea.

And although our memories of trip may fade, and all our snapshots are out of focus, we will still have the monthly credit card bills to remind us of our vacation.

Dean's Day

It's not a holiday yet, but I fully expect it to be one soon.

You always remember where you were on important days in your life, like the night you pulled away from the drive-in movie with the speaker still attached to the window. The day you first heard Sonny and Cher sing "I Got You Babe". The day Michael Jordan turned pro.

That's how it was Thursday, October 9, 1997, and that's why I'm sure some day it will be a holiday. At least a National Day of Mourning.

I walked outside to get the paper about 6:00 a.m. It's dark at that time of day in October and I remember looking up and seeing no stars in the morning sky. That should have been a warning to me.

When I picked up the paper I could see the headlines even in the dark. They weren't Pearl Harbor sized headlines, but they were close.

"Dean Smith to retire from basketball."

I rushed inside and woke up Sandra. Being an N.C. State Wolfpack fan, Sandra was not quite as excited as I was over the news, nor was she excited over being awakened at that hour. She couldn't even read the headlines in the dark like I could and I was forced to turn on the light. Somehow I was not in any mood to be in the light. It was a dark day.

I turned on the television, but they gave only a passing mention of the rumor.

"Boy, you see what they think of Dean," marveled Sandra, sliding a little dig in.

I wouldn't have done that to her, but then I couldn't remember who the Wolfpack's coach was for that month.

By the time I started my drive to work, the fog had started to settle in on the countryside. Appropriate, I thought. It will probably never be sunny again.

I needed consoling badly, so I called a friend, getting his wife instead. His marriage is also a mixed one, except that his wife is one of those dreaded ABC (Anyone But Carolina) fans. She was of little solace, but then she had once stood and cheered for the Romanian National Team against our beloved Heels. She did, however, give me Bob's car phone number and I called him in Charlotte.

"It's truly a dark day," he said, the traffic in Charlotte in the background. He didn't even seem to mind my having his cellular phone number, an item most of my friends would rather give out to the Mafia than to me.

Later in the day I heard that Robert Wilkie of Liberty's BB&T along with Liberty school teacher Ted Crutchfield were both under suicide watch. I called Teddy and commensurated with him for a few minutes. He was philosophical, saying that he understood that Dean needed more time with his family.

Heck, I thought I was his family.

Clemson Tiger fan Barry Cox noted that he had heard Dean had quit to get a nose job. Duke fan Tommy Johnson said that Dean couldn't stand all the "young guns" in the ACC any longer, that they didn't respect him like they should.

I told Barry that perhaps now Clemson could beat Carolina in Chapel Hill, something they hadn't managed to do in the history of the world. And I told Tommy that I hoped we didn't do to Bill Guthridge what Duke did to their assistant who took over for Coach K for a year and now is with the Peace Corps.

I had to laugh at the rumors that Dean didn't get along with Carolina's new athletic director, or that he and the new chancellor didn't see eye to eye.

Those rumors reminded me of the preacher who couldn't get along with God. In that case, who leaves? And I found it humorous that some sports writers felt that Dean went out now in order to push his old friend Bill Guthridge into the head coaching slot.

Dean could have tapped me as head coach and the university would have accepted it.

No, it's obvious that Dean is not in bad health, nor does he have any problems getting along with anyone at Carolina. Dean is Carolina.

First we lost Charles Kuralt and I am still in mourning. Now Dean. I don't know if I can take much more heartache.

Thanksgiving: The Real Story

You may think, like most Americans, that our Thanksgiving holiday tradition began in Massachusetts in the 1620's. Recent research, however, suggests that the original Thanksgiving dinner was actually served many years earlier and in the state of North Carolina.

This revelation may lead to many changes in history books and to new North Carolina license plates: "First in Thanksgiving"and "N.C. is for Turkeys".

I came across this in recent research at the North Carolina State Archives in Raleigh. An article in an old, yellowed newspaper caught my eye, the headline "Ancient Cranberry Relish Found in Montgomery County" jumping out at me like an alley cat on leftover broccoli casserole. You must remember that this was an OLD newspaper from the days when newspapers actually did contain local news in them.

As I read the story of an archaeological dig in Montgomery County, things started to fall into place. I had read earlier of an account of a Buck Private Bubba Barlowe, a soldier with Sir Walter Raleigh's expeditions, which had been published in the literary journal Soybean Digest. This, plus the obscure newspaper article on the findings in Montgomery County, convinced me that the first Thanksgiving actually occurred in North Carolina.

Barlowe told of an expedition, lead by Sir Walter Raleigh in the summer of 1584, during which the men became desperately lost and had to spend the winter "near Uwharrie with the Heathern Bis-Coe Indians." The troop had originally been sent by the Queen of England to explore Virginia and to "bring back Smithfield Hams and Lotterie Tickets", but somehow the expedition went farther south than planned.

Barlowe tells of traveling past a place he called Granganimeo which has been translated by scholars from the Algonquian as meaning "the land of many McDonald's" in which he said the natives chewed a plant called "Tobacco" and worshipped a god called NASCAR. The group, he later says, wanted to camp on Deep River, "but the Smells of Foul Sewage drove us deeper South".

Here Barlowe found the "Aire refreshing", this being a time before the discovery of chicken houses and a moratorium having been placed on hog parlors. But winter was setting in and Raleigh and his men soon realized that the territory they had wandered into had little or no provision for snow removal and no airports. So they were forced to settle in for the winter.

There they battled boredom by watching ACC football games and observing a crude, violent sport the Indians called "Wrassling".

This is bound to be the spot N.C.State Archaeologists discovered in the early 1960's. Scientists report uncovering a great amount of turkey salad, whipped sweet potatoes, cornbread dressing, several packs of Tums and the aforementioned cranberry relish at a site in Montgomery County. Very nearby a TV Guide, recliner and wide screen TV were excavated.

Barlowe says in his journal that the Englishmen nearly starved at this place until one day near the end of November when the local Indians showed up "With so Much Food in Plastic Bowles that we were Overwhelmed and could Bearly Watch the Football Game for all the Eating."

The English were so surprised and delighted by this gesture of friendship by the Indians that they decided to convert the entire tribe to Christianity, placing Bibles in all their motel rooms and building Baptist churches on every corner. Later, before returning to their ship, Raleigh's men killed off most of the tribe, burned the village, spoiled the crops and left the survivors small gold crosses to wear around their necks and a carton of religious tracts.

Barlowe, by the way, returned to the area in 1586 and noted that 'The Baptists here are thicker than Possums and Fight Amongst Themselves Like Children."

Sir Walter Raleigh, of course, managed to find his way back to Norfolk to the shipyard where he noted that the women on shore continued to invite the sailors "To Rest in Their Houses."

On returning to England, the men were so enthusiastic over their discovery of the cigarette business and the advertising revenue it would bring in that they completely forgot the story of North Carolina's first Thanksgiving.

But it can now be told that North Carolina hosted that very first special Thanksgiving and at a place very near us. And even though Raleigh's dream of bringing Christianity failed in much of the area, he succeeded in starting a tradition that has lasted to this very day and a large antacid industry to boot.

Thanksgiving Dinner

Thanksgiving is one of the rare holidays with which few of us can find fault.

Other holidays may have pagan roots, or religious overtones that conflict with opposing religious beliefs. Some groups may resist Veterans Day because they feel that it glorifies war. Native Americans resent Columbus Day because if it hadn't been for Columbus...oh, well, you get the picture.

The fact remains that there is always someone against everything, but Thanksgiving is a holiday for everyone. Some of us may have more to be thankful for than others and some of us may have to strain to find something worthy of thanks and a sad few of us may feel that we have no Higher Being to thank, but in the final analysis, all of us can be thankful for something.

We usually alternate holidays between our families. Last Thanksgiving we decided to have my family over to our house because of two occurrences: 1. We had more room, having recently moved. 2. Temporary insanity.

We broke the news to my Mom around September, knowing we might need time to sell her on the idea since she had cooked Thanksgiving dinner for over umpteen years.

I don't think I have ever seen Mom jump up and click her heels together before, but she wasn't hurt and when she gained her composure, she said she thought she could make the sacrifice.

As Thanksgiving Day neared we made our plans. Sandra decided that she would be in charge of cooking the turkey, mashing the potatoes, cooking the green beans, making the dressing, the tea, the gravy, browning the rolls and anything else that needed cooking.

I would be in charge of moving the TV to the den so we could watch football after the meal.

And I would be on alert, ready to go at a moment's notice to the grocery store should we need any last minute items.

I made four emergency trips to the store and met several people whose turkeys hadn't yet thawed either. When your turkey hasn't thawed, you can place it in cold water, but don't just take my word for it. It's written right there on the turkey. I guess they're born like that, with directions and all.

On one trip we needed a browning bag. Buy your browning bags early because they go fast. They come two to a pack, though, which is smart packaging, considering most of us only cook one turkey for Thanksgiving.

Of course, you are familiar with the origins of Thanksgiving. The Pilgrims, having mistakenly landed in a state none of them could spell, causing much distress for school children ever after, were close to starvation. The town board had turned down zoning for a fast food joint, the all-night grocery had not yet come to town and things were looking desperate.

The nearby Indian population saved the day by showing the Pilgrims how to grow corn, make jack-o-lanterns and play bingo.

The Pilgrims, who were growing mighty tired of eating hickory nuts and poke salad, were extremely thankful for the Indians help and decided to honor them with a feast.

It had been a good year, with low taxes, (although they hadn't received their vehicle tax, vehicles not being invented yet).

So, they invited the chief for Thanksgiving dinner, although it wasn't called Thanksgiving dinner until 1863 when President Lincoln designated it so, and by then we had begun to show our gratitude to the Indians by removing their race from the face of the earth and naming football teams for them.

Well, the Indian chief misunderstood the invitation and brought along a small band of 90 of his in-laws. This was definitely a case of not enough chiefs and too many Indians.

Luckily, the Indians brought venison, turkey and popcorn to the feast and saved the Pilgrims an emergency trip to the store. The popcorn was wasted since there were no football games to watch after dinner. And to this day, browning bags come two to a package in case so many Indians show up that you need more turkeys.

Our Thanksgiving Day went fine, with Sandra cooking a great feast, one to surely rival that first Thanksgiving dinner.

Our turkey thawed and turned out wonderful. I carved it and the slices looked like they had been gnawed off by a beaver. I also did a competent job moving the TV and some of us watched football and some of us slept.

And just to make it complete, my brother brought along three little Indians.

It was just like old times.

Watching Football With Fuseballs

When the Carolina Panthers began their first season in the NFL playoffs by hosting the hated Dallas Cowboys, we invited several couples over to watch the game. It didn't dawn on me until much later that this might have been a mistake.

I enjoy pro football, especially the Panthers. My life doesn't rise and fall with every Panther victory or loss (as it does with Carolina basketball) but I do pull for them unabashedly. And I root for them in spite of once being a lifelong Washington Redskin fan.

It never occurred to me that the friends I'd invite over to watch The Game might not want to watch the game.

The friends arrived right at game time. Although they looked well-fed at the time, it would soon be apparent that they hadn't eaten in days.

Everyone settled into their respective positions in front of the TV. The sound was adjusted so that it wouldn't interfere with any conversation that might be going on because, besides being hungry, this crowd hadn't seen each other in months and had a lot of news to catch up on.

As the teams waited for the kickoff, a cry went up in the living room for popcorn. As the designated popcorn popper, I headed for the kitchen.

Theater owners, being wise in the ways of consumers, have their popcorn already popped. This is so that they, too, can watch the movie if they wish.

I popped all the popcorn Orville had to offer and even broke out some of the Healthy-for-You brand. The party bunch ate it all, even the low fat stuff.

Next, they called for napkins and drinks, which I delivered in between trying to watch plays.

"We're not doing too good," someone announced when I finally got seated, sometime in the second quarter.

The screen showed the Panthers leading 7-0.

"We're winning," I said. "When did we score a touchdown?"

"That was us?" someone asked. "I thought it was the Falcons."

"Cowboys," I corrected. "I bet everyone in Charlotte is going crazy."

"Charlotte?" someone else asked. "Does Charlotte have a team?"

"Of course they do," another friend answered. "It's the Hornets."

"Do you have any chips and dip?" another friend wanted to know.

The conversation swung to the Panther's mascot, Sir Purr. Someone had read that a fan in High Point had bought season tickets to the Panther's games and wore a panther suit to them.

Was he the mascot, they wanted to know and, if so, why did he have to buy his own outfit?

The odd thing about the conversation was that whenever commercials came on, the crowd became strangely quiet. I mentioned this in light of the fact that the game was almost to halftime and I had seen and heard about three plays.

"The commercials are interesting," I was informed by someone whose mouth was full of popcorn. I privately hoped it was the heathy stuff.

At halftime, the Panthers were leading.

"We're not doing too good," a friend announced, heading for the bathroom. "That one guy isn't even dribbling the ball. Don't you have to dribble?"

Most of the halftime, like the commercials, was eerily quiet. But just as soon as the second half began, the conversation picked up.

Someone asked how the Panther owner Jerry Richardson had made his fortune. Another friend told him that he had owned the fast food chain called Hardees.

The rest of the second half was spent wondering who the North Carolina lieutenant governor was who once owned Hardees. Finally, about the time the game was over, it was decided that it was Jim Gardner.

Luckily, the Panthers won, albeit without any visible support or much attention from my group.

"Maybe we'll have better luck next time," one said as we headed out the door for pizza.

Yeah, I thought to myself. I'll tape the game next year and watch it while everyone else has gone for pizza. That way I won't miss out on all the conversation.

Flag Fad

It always amazes me how fads crop up. Just as soon as you think you've got one fad whipped, up pops another one.

It used to be flamingos in the yard and you still see some of them yet.

Then it was cows, herds of cows, and deer, too. And ducks with clothes on, even. Before all this it was live chickens and guineas, which were harder to care for, but good as an early warning system. Especially the guineas.

Then people started putting wreathes on their doors even when it wasn't Christmas. You could have your Thanksgiving wreath, then the ever-popular Christmas wreath, and after that a Valentine's wreath and a Spring wreath and so on and so forth. Needless to say, this was a big boon to the wreath industry.

But now the fad seems to be flags.

I don't know where the flags came from. Maybe someone knows the history of this thing, but I don't. It was probably just like the hula hoop, it just appeared one day. The first one I saw was the pineapple flag, which is supposed to signify hospitality, so maybe the flags originated in Hawaii. Or maybe the pineapple industry spawned the whole thing.

Flags, or banners as those in the know call them, seem to have originated in Persia, where a blacksmith's apron was waved to urge on troops in battle. As far as national flags go, Denmark's has been flying the longest, seven hundred years. Naval ships routinely used banners to signal other ships at sea.

Flags on doorways of homes all seem to have a special meaning, most known only to the owners of the flags or to those who are more in the know than I am.

Take the pineapple for instance. At first, I though it meant that the home owner was a tad fruity. Or maybe some Polynesians had moved in. Or that they had served one too many pineapple daiquiris.

How are we supposed to know that this means "hospitality"? Is there some kind of guidebook available? And can you walk right in on these hospitable homes if you need, say, a cold drink or to use the bathroom? Do the homeowners walk around in the middle of the day wearing grass skirts? The whole thing is confusing to me.

I can understand some of these flags. There's the jack-o-lantern for Halloween and a turkey for Thanksgiving (either that, or the wife is making a statement about her husband). There are also flags for Easter, Veteran's Day, Valentine's, Groundhog Day, winter, spring, summer, fall, Dog Days, etc. Boy, these flag people knew a good thing when they saw it.

One popular flag is the college team banner. Folks have been flying these on their cars for several years and now they've spread to the subdivisions. On a given Saturday morning you can see cars zooming past flying the flags of such football powerhouses as N.C. State, Wake Forest and Duke. Then later that night you can see the same cars sneaking back into town, flags either at half mast or disposed of earlier in the trash. I suggest that these fans break out the more prudent basketball flag.

Riding around recently, I easily spotted many homes with flags flying. There were several which sported a TV and a potato on their banners, which I guessed meant the husband was home on the couch.

I saw one with the skull and crossbones featured on it which I figured meant that the in-laws were visiting. There was one of a house with flames shooting out of the windows, which I guess meant someone had cooked. There were several upside down banners, an international signal of distress or impending divorce. I saw one flag with a golf club on it (husband playing golf) and another with a shopping bag (wife out shopping). Another had a broken piggy bank (kid in college). There were several that said only "No Trespassing."

So far we have resisted this flag fad, although Sandra has mentioned flying one with a stove and red line through it.

Happy Birthday, You Old Coot

We've had a rash of birthdays around our house lately, some more pleasant than others. Birthdays are OK, I guess, considering the alternative, but if you've seen one, you've seen them all.

After you reach a certain age, you start getting cards like "I once saw someone your age," Inside, over a picture of a mummy, it reads "But I quit going to the museum." Or "I got you a regular card because I know irregularity is a problem at your age."

There's a whole card industry built around making old people miserable for their birthday.

It wasn't always like that. The celebration of birthdays supposedly originated in Europe many years ago and soon spread throughout the entire known world and parts of Kansas. Many of the original customs were carried down to this very day with some modification.

For instance, the first person known to celebrate a birthday was overcome from trying to blow out the Yule log after making a wish. Soon after this, candles were invented.

Nowadays, we do about the same thing. First, you go by the fire department and get the permit. Then you make sure there's plenty of ventilation. And you need help because there's no way you can light all those candles by yourself before the first ones burn out. Then you're eating more wax than cake which is awfully hard to clean out of your dentures.

I actually had a birthday party not too long ago during which the cake was ruined because of the heat from the candles. Party goers determined that this was due to: 1. Too many candles 2. Too little breath from birthday boy.

Early birthday celebrations began with the belief that evil spirits gathered around a person who was celebrating a birthday. People believed that if this person was surrounded by relatives and friends their good wishes would help ward off the evil beings. One bright celebrant suggested to his friends that their bringing gifts might ward off these spirits even more.

I have noticed that at my birthday parties, it is mighty difficult to tell the evil spirits from the friends and relatives.

At first, only prominent people were beset by birthday celebrations. Then the card companies decided to let everyone in on the fun.

Germans were the first people to celebrate their children's birthdays with a party called Kinderfeste which, loosely translated, means "Mother's nightmare" or "Cake on der Karpet".

Present birthday parties are not much different than the originals. Now evil friends and relatives surround the person celebrating the birthday in hopes of warding off any happiness that person might accidently incur.

The going thing now is to honor the birthday person by humiliating them as much as possible. One neat way of doing this is by placing a photo of the poor honoree in the paper. This can be any picture taken in the third grade after a rain storm. Or, for women, any photo in hair curlers. A favorite for men is anything in women's lingerie. Underneath this squirrelly-looking likeness is usually a funny, original quote, such as "Lordy, Lordy, look who's forty", which doesn't rhyme, but is better than "Ain't it nifty, look who's fifty."

I expect to look in the paper someday and see the picture of some scrubby headed kid in a plaid shirt and a cutline that reads: "Ready for the Pearly gate, Poor Claude is 108."

Or there's the practice of renting a portable sign and placing it near a heavily traveled road. These read something like "Mozelle's nearly dead, Tomorrow she's a hundred. Love, your family."

My friends rented a sign for one of my birthdays, but misplaced the letters. This is why it's prudent to have older friends. Their minds go first.

Some places of business give their employees a day off on their birthday. Believe me, this is a necessity after the degradation and disparagement your average birthday party brings.

And if you're lucky enough to miss all the pictures, cards, and signs, you're just likely to be the recipient of a belly dancing exhibition by a mostly naked person half your age. Afterwards, for at least forty or fifty years, your spouse will accuse you daily of having arranged the belly dancer yourself.

I long for the good old days of birthday parties of cake and ice cream and pin the tail on the donkey when everyone went outside afterwards and merely gouged each others eyes out.

It's Hard to be a Potato Without a Couch

There is nothing like getting a day off and sitting on the front porch watching the world go by with nary a care in the world. But this is mighty hard to do on today's porch furniture. The stuff is too stiff, too rigid, too hard. To relax on the porch, you need a good couch or arm chair.

You may have missed the news, but the town of Wilson, N.C., has banned indoor furniture on porches.

No more couches on the front porch. No more porch sofas. No more La-Z-Boys. No more Barcaloungers.

This may seem like a small thing to you, this outlawing of ottomans, this deportation of divans. But each small erosion of our rights leads to bigger and bigger excesses by government until one day we awake and we're speaking Russian and wearing little furry caps.

Oh, I know they say that Communism is dead, but they forget that Cuba is still just 90 miles from Miami. And I'll guarantee you those Cubans don't allow anything comfortable on their porches, either.

Today they take our settees; tomorrow they'll want the hogs out of our front yards. Where will it end?

I'll bet Thomas Jefferson, who was known to enjoy a Sunday afternoon sprawled out on the front seat from a '55 Chevy on his porch at Monticello, is spinning in his grave.

A group called the Wilson Appearance Commission is the group that first recommended that indoor furniture, because it is prone to get wet and moldy, be deemed a public nuisance. This furniture, they said, also represented a health hazard, becoming a breeding place for rats and fleas.

"There could be some family health problems from the weatherization of the couch," said Wilson's Planning Director Jim Bradshaw.

The use of the word "weatherization" by Mr. Bradshaw, by the way, shows some devious socialistic influence.

At the very least, he's received a postcard from Russia sometime in his life, because nobody down South says "weatherization". We might say "that couch is slicker than a pot of boiled okra" but never "weatherization". Besides, if Mr. Bradshaw wants family health problems, wait till everybody in the family comes down with bad backs and ends up at the chiropractor's from sitting on those hard, straight back chairs.

Dan Carter, a professor of Southern history at Emory University has called the ban on porch sofas "an act of community destruction".

Carter probably recalls the British attempt to ban washing machines from porches that led directly to the Revolutionary War.

The front porch is an extremely important part of Southern culture. Front porches are no longer required on homes in the South, but at one time they were mandatory.

Every Sunday afternoon, folks would drag a chair or two from the house and sit on the porch, just enjoying the day and each other's company and waving at whoever passed by.

This was before the advent of television when it became illegal to enjoy each other's company.

What more comfortable way to enjoy a Sunday afternoon than the plush luxury of a couch? The fact that the couch got wet every now and then was of no concern because it always dried out eventually. And as one Wilson citizen was heard to say, "It certainly ain't gonna dry out sitting inside."

But the invention of air conditioning and the aforementioned television have almost made the front porch extinct. If you ride by a home today and see someone sitting on the porch, you know one of two things:

1. Their power is off.

2. Their spouse is mad at them.

But if you see a couch or two on the front porch, you know this is a family that enjoys each other's company. This is a home built for comfort, not just appearances. These are folks who, when you ride by, will wave at you whether they know you or not.

Today's porch furniture is uncomfortable and stiff. It looks pretty, but who sits on it? No self-respecting chicken is going to lay an egg on it, that's for sure. And you'll never see a hound dog curled up on it, either.

I certainly hope the citizens of Wilson will rise up and stop this foolishness before it gets out of hand.

Let them take our couches away and what's next? Our Frigidaires?

A Room For All Seasons

Willard had come over to the house under the pretense of wanting to help me organize the stuff in my out building. There is no greater gift a man can give than to offer to help a friend straighten out his stuff. I suspected, however, that Willard actually wanted to attempt to recover some of the tools I had borrowed from him over the years.

I welcomed the help, though, since Sandra had wanted the building cleaned out for the longest time, using the flimsy excuse that "you couldn't find anything in it."

It had never dawned on me that you needed to find the stuff. It was a storage building, not a findage building.

We picked a fairly pleasant summer day to start working on the clean up. When I opened the two doors of the storage building, Willard gasped.

"I've never seen so many Christmas decorations," he marveled, peering into the building. "And Thanksgiving decorations and Easter bunnies and Fourth of July arrangements...where did you get all this stuff?"

"You never know when a holiday is going to pop up," I said. "You've got to be prepared."

Willard's astonishment reminded me of the times my Aunt Ellen Dixon Clark would come up from Augusta to visit family and stay in Pittsboro with Mammaw (my grandmother, her mother). Mammaw would always put her up in the spare bedroom.

"You never knew what season you were going to wake up in," Aunt Ellen said of the bedroom. "There was a Christmas tree in one corner with a funeral wreath leaning against it, an Easter rabbit in another corner, a Thanksgiving turkey on the chest of drawers. You really had to think a minute after you woke up to try to remember what time of year it was."

Sometimes Aunt Ellen would wake up in the middle of the summer humming "Jingle Bells".

Mammaw was prepared for any occasion. When Christmas came, she just reached into the spare bedroom and pulled out the Christmas tree, pre-decorated from years past, dusted it off and set it in the living room.

I told Willard that was my family's strength. We were always ready for a holiday.

We began moving stuff out of the building into the yard. It was a lot like cleaning out a closet. We found ourselves spending more time looking at things than cleaning.

"There's actually a lawn mower in here," Willard said in wonderment.

After awhile we had Christmas trees, wreathes, wrapping paper, snowmen, angels, reindeer, Fourth of July arrangements complete with American flags, Easter bunnies and chicks and ceramic jack-o-lanterns stacked up in the yard. Then we discovered the ice cream freezer.

"We usually bring this out on the Fourth of July," I told Willard. "That's why these quilts are stuffed back in the corner. We spread them out on the ground, lie around and eat homemade ice cream all afternoon."

Willard looked at me and I looked at Willard. We knew at that moment that great minds think alike.

He rode downtown and brought back a couple of bags of ice and ice cream salt. I had the recipe for vanilla ice cream mixed, ready and waiting in the freezer when he got back. We plugged in the freezer, packed in the ice and salt and laid back on the quilts waiting for the motor to quit. It didn't take long for it to freeze and soon we were enjoying homemade ice cream.

"It was better when we turned it ourselves," Willard noted.

"Yeah," I replied, "My fifth bowl wasn't frozen quite as hard as it should have been"

About that time Sandra pulled into the driveway and saw Willard and me lying on the quilts among the Christmas trees, holly wreathes, Wisemen, angels, Santa Clauses, American flags and Easter bunnies.

She got out of the car, shook her head, and disappeared inside the house.

"You know," said Willard, "if everyday were a holiday, we would never get old."

"Then you and I, my friend," I replied, "should live forever."